DELTA Business Communication Skills

Series Editors
Susan Lowe and Louise Pile

Business English Language Practice

GRAMMAR AND VOCABULARY

Susan Lowe and Louise Pile

DELTA Publishing
Quince Cottage
Hoe Lane
Peaslake
Surrey GU5 9SW
England

www.deltapublishing.co.uk

First published 2009

Edited by Catriona Watson-Brown
Designed by Caroline Johnston
Illustrations by CartoonStock
Cover design by Peter Bushell
Printed in Spain by Grafo, S.A.

ISBN 978-1-905085-29-3

Contents

Introduction

The *DELTA Business Communication Skills* series uses a learner-centred approach to develop key communication and language skills essential for today's international business environment. The series is designed for learners of business English at pre-intermediate and intermediate level, either pre-service or in-service, and it can be used either in the classroom or for self-study.

Business English Language Practice aims to support the other books in the series by developing grammar and vocabulary skills. It is split into two sections – **Grammar** and **Vocabulary** – each containing 12 units, which focus on the key areas covered in the rest of the series.

- The **Grammar** section covers meaning, plus use and form.
- The **Vocabulary** section covers meaning, spelling, pronunciation, collocations and word families.

Each unit has a **Practice** section and a **Reference** section.

The book also contains:

- **Needs analysis**. This encourages you to consider what you need to focus on in order to get the most out of the book and your learning.
- **Learning journal**. This provides the opportunity to reflect and personalize what you have studied in the book.
- **Answer key**. This is designed to enable you to work either alone or with a teacher.

How to use this book

Step 1

Start by working through the **Needs analysis** (pages 5–6). This will help you to:

- consider your strengths and weaknesses in English grammar and business vocabulary;
- identify and practise your immediate and future needs for grammar and vocabulary;
- determine the order in which you work through the units in this book.

Step 2

Familiarize yourself with the **Learning journal** (page 7), to which you are asked to refer at the end of every Practice section.

Step 3

Work through the units in the order you feel most appropriate to your needs and interests.

We hope you enjoy using this book.

S. Lowe   Pile

Susan Lowe and Louise Pile
Authors

About the authors

Susan Lowe and Louise Pile have extensive general and business English teaching and teacher-training experience. They have written and edited a range of print and multimedia language-learning materials.

Needs analysis

Consider how effective you are in business grammar and vocabulary by answering the questions below and on the next page. Choose the correct options to complete the sentences. Then check your answers on page 74 and work through the *Prioritizing your needs* section on page 6.

Grammar

Present tenses

1 My boss ———— work before 7 a.m. at least twice a week.

   a starts **b** is starting **c** does start

2 At the moment, sales ———— very quickly.

   a increase **b** are increasing **c** increased

Past tenses

3 Only six people ———— the training yesterday.

   a attend **b** are attending **c** attended

4 What ———— at your appraisal last week?

   a did you discuss **b** you discuss **c** do you discuss

Will and going to

5 Are you late? ———— you a lift to work if you like.

   a I'll give **b** I give **c** I giving

6 It's already decided. We ———— the conference in May this year.

   a are going to hold **b** held **c** hold

Modals

7 I'm not sure what to do about the meeting. I ———— just postpone it.

   a can **b** shall **c** might

8 Stop here. You ———— go into the chemical research lab.

   a don't need to **b** mustn't **c** couldn't

Conditionals

9 If I were you, I ———— for the job.

   a would apply **b** apply **c** applied

10 If sales ———— further, the company will be in trouble.

   a will fall **b** fall **c** are falling

–ing forms and infinitives

11 My colleague suggested ———— out for lunch.

   a to go **b** go **c** going

12 Are you hoping ———— promotion?

   a to get **b** getting **c** get

Comparatives and superlatives

13 James is much ———— at finance than Henry.

   a good **b** better **c** well

14 The Oxford branch is ———— successful in the whole company.

   a the more **b** more **c** the most

Relative clauses

15 My boss, ———— is the head of HR, is planning to retire early.

   a who **b** which **c** that

16 The department ———— I work in is under tremendous pressure.

   a what **b** that **c** who

Articles

17 Have you seen ———— report we were talking about earlier?

   a the **b** a **c** —

18 I'm ———— designer and I work for Shiptons.

   a an **b** a **c** the

Determiners

19 I'm sorry, but I don't have ———— money on me.

   a some **b** any **c** many

20 Don't worry. We've still got ———— time left before the meeting.

   a a little **b** little **c** few

Passives

21 Due to a lack of support, the exhibition ———— .

   a has been cancelled **b** has cancelled **c** cancelled

22 All staff reaching their target ———— a bonus.

   a will give **b** will be given **c** give

Reported speech

23 My boss told me she ———— her job.

   a would hate **b** hating **c** hated

24 Sylvie said she ———— to take early retirement.

   a wanted **b** will want **c** want

Vocabulary

Companies and offices

1 KP Recruitment hasn't been in business for very long. It is _____ company.

    a an upcoming   **b** a well-established   **c** a multinational

2 The media are reporting the unexpected _____ between JG Construction plc and DesignIt.

    a merge   **b** merger   **c** merged

Finance

3 Sales have continued to go down over the last few months – they've _____ to 10,000 units per month.

    a dropped   **b** increased   **c** evened out

4 We don't make much money on those products, but we do on the E754 – it's quite _____ .

    a profit   **b** profitable   **c** profitably

Human resources

5 Helmut is only 59, but he's already planning what he'll do during his _____ .

    a retirement   **b** pension   **c** application

6 JP Electronics looks after its staff – all _____ have good salaries and opportunities for training.

    a employees   **b** employers   **c** employment

Logistics

7 The goods are being loaded onto the lorry, about to be _____ .

    a delivered   **b** dispatched   **c** ordered

8 Our usual _____ has let us down, so we are looking for a new one.

    a supply   **b** supplier   **c** supplies

Meetings and conferences

9 Linda took notes in the meeting, so she is typing up the _____ .

    a minutes   **b** handouts   **c** agenda

10 Are you able to _____ the meeting tomorrow?

    a attendance   **b** attendee   **c** attend

People and places

11 The Head of Production speaks to workers on the _____ every day.

    a office   **b** factory   **c** shop floor

12 Helen currently _____ a team of 12 people.

    a manages   **b** managers   **c** managed

Planning

13 We should not open any more offices. However, we need to _____ and produce a wider range of goods.

    a downsize   **b** diversify   **c** expand

14 Next year's results aren't _____ – we had good results last year, but bad ones this year.

    a predictable   **b** predict   **c** prediction

Production and processes

15 Eduardo earns more money if he works the night _____ .

    a stock   **b** shift   **c** batch

16 We're planning to _____ more to meet demand.

    a produce   **b** product   **c** production

Projects and teams

17 Have we got a _____ ? We need to know the start and end dates for the project.

    a specification   **b** deadline   **c** schedule

18 Before starting the project, we need _____ of costs.

    a estimate   **b** an estimation   **c** estimated

Sales and marketing

19 We're _____ the advertising campaign in May this year.

    a promoting   **b** inquiring   **c** launching

20 GlobePharm plc is reducing its prices to remain _____ .

    a compete   **b** competition   **c** competitive

Telephone and e-mailing

21 I'm on a train. If I _____ , I'll call you back.

    a get cut off   **b** get through   **c** leave a message

22 Please refer to the prices in the _____ document.

    a attach   **b** attachment   **c** attached

Training

23 How many _____ are there on each day of the training course?

    a programmes   **b** exams   **c** sessions

24 This course should help participants _____ writing skills.

    a develop   **b** development   **c** developed

Prioritizing your needs

Step 1

Each unit of *Business English Language Practice* focuses on a different area. After you have completed the Needs analysis, look at the contents page and think about which areas you need to work on. Developing your awareness of what you already do well and what you could do better will allow you to focus on improving those skills you really need.

Step 2

Note down the units you would like to work through in order of priority for you, in terms of the area in which you feel the weakest (using your answers to the questions on this page and page 5 as a guide), or which is currently of most importance to you. If necessary, discuss and agree this with your teacher.

Priority	Unit and focus area
1	
2	
3	
4	
5	
6	

Step 3

Before you start working through the units – in the order you have decided on – look at the Learning journal on page 7.

Learning journal

During the course As you work through each unit, summarize helpful language (grammar and/or vocabulary) from each unit. An example is given, but what you note down will depend upon your own learning pattern.

> **Unit:**
>
> **Useful language:**

Example

> **Unit:** Articles
>
> **Useful language:**
> 'America', but 'the USA'
> I am a web editor.
> Can I speak to the manager?

After the course It is important to consolidate your learning, both during the course and afterwards at work. After you have completed each unit, you should decide how you will continue to develop your language skills, for example which practice exercises you will do or which reference sections you need to look at again. Note that it is helpful to give yourself realistic deadlines! Make notes, for example using a framework like the one below.

> **Unit:**
>
> **I need to:**
>
> **To do this better, I intend to:**

Example

> **Unit:** Projects and teams
>
> **I need to:**
> be able to talk about projects to clients and my team members
>
> **To do this better, I intend to:**
> – do all the practice exercises again in the next two weeks.
> – use five of the words and phrases at the team meeting next month.

This book is designed to be used during and after a course, so keep it with you and refer back to it whenever you need to, and keep adding to your notes!

Present tenses

 Before you do these exercises, look at page 56 of the Reference section.

Form: Present simple

I Complete the advertisement using the correct form of the verbs in brackets.

◾ 1 _____ (you/want) to improve your telephone skills?

◾ 2 _____ (you/often/feel) nervous about giving a presentation?

The company PTL 3 _____ (provide) one-to-one tuition. Delegates often 4 _____ (say) how much they 5 _____ (value) the individual support they 6 _____ (receive) from the experienced trainers.

◾ 7 _____ (you/work) for a small company?

We 8 _____ (not/just/offer) face-to-face training, and our work 9 _____ (not/only/involve) large businesses. Each month, we also 10 _____ (run) courses for employees of small firms and individuals. Before a course, our head trainer always 11 _____ (meet) clients and 12 _____ (find) out what their needs are.

> The -s ending of third person singular present simple forms can be pronounced in three ways: /z/ *finds*, /s/ *works* and /ɪz/ *rises*.

Form: Present continuous

2 Complete the conversation using the correct form of the verbs in brackets.

Bipun: Hi, Atul. Good to see you again. 1 _____ (you/give) the keynote speech?

Atul: No, I 2 _____ (not/do) that. I 3 _____ (just/lead) a workshop.

Bipun: Oh, really? I 4 _____ (work) on the exhibition stand this morning, but I 5 _____ (not/plan) to be here after 1 p.m. 6 _____ (you/do) anything at lunchtime?

Atul: Not really. Let's meet up.

Bipun: Sure. Anyway, who 7 _____ (you/work) for these days?

Atul: I'm still at Xcom, although I 8 _____ (not/manage) the same project any more. I 9 _____ (now/run) a project to develop new DVD-based toys. The company 10 _____ (face) increased competition, so who knows how long I'll be there!

Bipun: It's the same for me. We 11 _____ (not/sell) as many TV games as we used to. The market 12 _____ (change), but the company 13 _____ (not/keep) up with these changes.

> When forming the present participle, check your spelling – verbs ending in *-e* drop the final *-e* before adding *-ing* (e.g. *providing*).

Use: Routine events / events happening now

3 Put the words in the correct order to form sentences. Then decide whether each sentence describes:

a routine activities   b events happening around now

1 you / get / lift / work / Do / usually / a / to / ?

2 taking / just / Sally's / tea / a / break

3 moment / Manchester / not / in / the / We're / living / at

4 pay / rises / often / get / Employees / don't / very

5 most / Staff / days / start / at / work / 7.30 a.m.

6 doing / boss / What / your / is / right now / ?

4 a Write three sentences about what happens at your company using these phrases.

- every day
- at least twice a month
- never

b Write three sentences about what is happening at your company using these phrases.

- now
- currently
- this morning

Use: Temporary / permanent situations

5 Correct the errors in these sentences. Three of them do not contain errors. Then decide whether each sentence describes:
a temporary situations   b facts / permanent situations

1 The company I work for produces electrical equipment.

2 I work in the finance department for a few days.

3 We recruit for a new Marketing Manager at the moment.

4 My colleague's on leave, so I handle all his PR this week.

5 I'm helping out a colleague with this paperwork, as he's overwhelmed!

6 The TVs in this shop don't cost very much.

7 How many staff are you having?

8 I'm not belonging to any union.

Use: Future arrangements

6 Match the sentence halves.

1 What are you doing ...

2 We're moving ...

3 Mandy isn't going to the show this year ...

4 I'm attending a conference next Friday, ...

5 Why aren't we promoting our own products at ...

a ... after work on Friday?

b ... the July exhibition?

c ... because she's going on holiday that week.

d ... offices in the summer.

e ... so can we meet another time?

Consolidation

7 Write the verbs in brackets in the present simple or present continuous.

1 What _____ (you/do) next weekend?

2 Staff members usually _____ (take) their annual leave in July.

3 I _____ (not/understand) that. Can you explain it again, please?

4 We often _____ (use) financial consultants.

5 We _____ (recruit) a new Finance Manager at the moment.

6 Where _____ (you/come) from? Germany?

7 Jenna _____ (not/run) the course today. She's ill.

8 I really _____ (not/like) that idea.

 NOW TURN TO YOUR LEARNING JOURNAL AND MAKE NOTES ON THIS SECTION.

Past tenses

★ Before you do these exercises, look at page 56 of the Reference section.

Form: Past simple

1 Complete the sentences using the correct past simple form of the verbs in brackets.

1 When _____ you _____ your own business? (start)

2 Yesterday, I _____ _____ work until 9 p.m. (finish)

3 The engineer _____ over three hours trying to fix the photocopier. (spend)

4 I really _____ the presentation skills seminar last week. (enjoy)

5 The company _____ its profits by 15% last year. (increase)

6 The course _____ _____ as much as we expected. (cost)

7 Unfortunately, we _____ _____ the project on time. (complete)

8 My boss hates flying, so she _____ to Edinburgh by train. (go)

> See page 80 for a list of some common irregular verbs.

Form: Present perfect

2 Find and correct the errors in these sentences. Two of the sentences are correct.

1 I work at Colourlines since January.

2 How long you have been a consultant?

3 I haven't travelled abroad on business for two years.

4 I earned almost £1,000 in sales since June.

5 I'm sorry, I didn't start on the new project yet.

6 Martin and I have worked together on four projects this year.

7 How long do you know my boss?

8 My new employers haven't contact me recently about my starting date.

> The -ed ending is pronounced /ɪd/ in some verbs, /t/ in others and /d/ in others. Look in your dictionary to see how -ed is pronounced in the verbs from these exercises.

Use: Finished and unfinished time

3 What is the difference in meaning between the sentences in each pair?

1 a Did you enjoy your holiday in Scotland?
  b Have you enjoyed your holiday in Scotland?

2 a I didn't finish my application.
  b I haven't finished my application.

3 a I worked overseas for about ten years.
  b I have worked overseas for about ten years.

4 Match the sentence halves. Then decide whether each one describes events that:
A have finished   B started in the past and are continuing

1 My boss gave a speech last week ...

2 I haven't sent the e-mail yet about ...

3 The car broke down yesterday, ...

4 I didn't take my holiday ...

5 How many colleagues have you invited ...

6 Did you call ...

a ... in June, as the weather was bad.

b ... about economic developments.

c ... the printers before lunch as we agreed?

d ... to attend the marketing seminar?

e ... so I had to take the bus to work.

f ... the new HR policies.

Use: Time phrases

5 Complete the time phrases in the sentences using the words in the box. Which verbs are in the past simple? Which are in the present perfect?

| ago | already | already | ever | for | in | last | never | since | this | yet |

1 We only put a job advert in the local paper _____ week, and we've _____ had over 50 applicants.

2 I received the consultancy contract three days _____ , but I haven't had time to read it _____ .

3 Ginny has only worked here _____ a year, but she's _____ become a director.

4 'When did you join Steelcom?'
  'I've been here _____ 2001.'

5 'Have you _____ been to France?'
  'I've _____ been, but I'd love to go.'

6 I sent off three bids _____ June and I've already done two more _____ week.

www.CartoonStock.com

'For heaven's sake, Wilson!
Did I forget to send you home last night?'

Consolidation

6 Complete the e-mail using the correct form of the verbs in the box.

| be | come | get | not/hear | post | promise | not/receive |
| speak | tell | not/write | | | | |

For more on past tenses, see Exercise 2 on page 54 and the 'Spelling' section on page 73.

Hi Trudy

I'm afraid I [1] _____ all the reports yet. The production team [2] _____

me their report two weeks ago, and I [3] _____ the marketing team's on

Friday by e-mail. Marco from Sales [4] _____ me yesterday that he

[5] _____ his team's report yet. Apparently, he only [6] _____ back

from Paris on Wednesday and he [7] _____ really busy since then. Also, I

[8] _____ from Sam in Logistics. When I [9] _____ to him back in June,

he [10] _____ to send in his report in good time. Anyway, the result of

→ NOW TURN TO YOUR LEARNING JOURNAL AND MAKE NOTES ON THIS SECTION.

Will and *going to*

 Before you do these exercises, look at page 57 of the Reference section.

Form: *Will* and *going to*

See page 56 for how the present simple can be used to talk about schedules.

1 Choose the correct options.

1 We *'re going to / 're going* make a profit this year.

2 Why *he won't / won't he* come for lunch?

3 *Who's going / Who going* to lead the meeting today?

4 Wait for me. *I / I'll* just fetch my coat.

5 *Are you going / You going* to work late today?

6 *Shall / Will* I give you a hand?

7 I expect *I'll be / I be* in Barcelona tomorrow.

8 What *are we going to do / we do* about all this?

Use: Schedules

★ ★ ★ ★ ★ ★ ★ ★ ★ ★ ★
9.00 WELCOME
9.00–10.30 OPENING SPEECH
10.30–11.00 COFFEE BREAK
11.00–12.30 WORKSHOPS
12.30–1.30 LUNCH
1.30–3.00 WORKSHOPS
3.00–3.30 TEA BREAK
3.30–5.00 CLOSING SPEECH
★ ★ ★ ★ ★ ★ ★ ★ ★ ★ ★

2 Complete the e-mail about a conference using *will / won't* and the verbs in brackets.

Sally, please ¹_____ (you/let) staff know about the conference?

It ²_____ (begin) at nine with a welcome address by the Chair. Then there ³_____ (be) a speech by one of our trustees, followed by a break. This year, the morning and afternoon workshops ⁴_____ (not/last) two hours, but just 90 minutes, and they ⁵_____ (take) place in the main conference suite instead of the annexe. Lunch ⁶_____ (not/be) until 12.30. Also, the closing speech ⁷_____ (not/happen) unless we find a speaker. Any ideas?

Use: Spontaneous offers/decisions

3 Match the sentences.

1 That door keeps banging.

2 Gosh, this bag is heavy.

3 I'm tired – I'm off home.

4 My car won't start.

5 I've got a real headache.

6 It's Sian's last day on Friday.

a Don't worry, we'll call you a cab.

b Sorry, I'll shut it for you.

c Poor you – shall I get you some paracetamol?

d I think I'll join you.

e I didn't know. I'll get her a card.

f I'll carry it for you.

Use: Predictions

4 Make predictions about yourself and other people (e.g. your boss, a colleague, a friend) using *will / won't*.

1 (on the 20th of this month)   My boss definitely won't be at work on the 20th of this month – she'll be on holiday in Spain.

2 (tomorrow at 3 p.m.)

3 (Friday lunchtime)

4 (next summer)

5 (in five years' time)

Use: Plans

5 Write about things you or other people are/aren't planning to do over the next seven days using *going to*. Use these ideas.

- buy a computer
- ride a motorbike
- give a presentation
- eat pineapple
- go on a bus
- attend a meeting
- take a course
- start work early
- have a holiday
- buy a present

Example: My boss isn't going to buy a computer, but he is going to take a course.

Use: Predictions based on evidence

6 Match the sentences.

1 I didn't hear my alarm clock.
2 That screw looks a bit loose.
3 I feel so tired.
4 Interest rates are low.
5 It's been really cold for weeks
6 Are you really going to Geneva?
7 Whiteside is losing money.
8 The new server isn't very reliable.

a More people are going to buy a house.
b It's going to be a long winter.
c You're going to have to learn French.
d Management is going to make staff redundant.
e The company isn't going to get a new one, though.
f I'm not going to get to work on time.
g I'm going to fall asleep soon.
h Oh yes – do you think the chair's going to collapse?

Practise your pronunciation by reading the sentence pairs aloud. See page 62 for tips on linking sounds.

Consolidation

7 Complete the dialogues using the correct form of *will* / *going to*.

1 'Did you pick up the *Business Journal* for me?'
'Oh no, I forgot. I _____ go back for it now.'

2 'What about having a meeting on Friday about the project?'
'Good idea, I _____ ask my line manager if he's available.'

3 'Are you both leaving already?'
'Yes, we _____ to visit a client.'

4 'Have you booked your flight yet?'
'No, I think I _____ do it later once I've checked prices.'

5 'Why have you booked the Hotel Magnifico for next week?'
'We _____ launch a new product there.'

6 'What _____ wear to the office dinner?'
'I'm not sure yet.'

7 'Did you see the training course brochure?'
'Yes, I _____ do the presentation skills course.'

8 'Shall we all go out for lunch?'
'I'm afraid Jason and I _____ attend an exhibition.'

9 'Did you speak to Jenny?'
'Whoops! I forgot. I _____ phone her now.'

→ NOW TURN TO YOUR LEARNING JOURNAL AND MAKE NOTES ON THIS SECTION.

Modals

 Before you do these exercises, look at page 57 of the Reference section.

Form: Modals

1 Find and correct the errors in these sentences. Two of the sentences are correct.

1 May I to use your phone, please?

2 You don't have come to the exhibition.

3 You mustn't stay late tonight.

4 Jack coulds help us, I think.

5 My boss doesn't can speak French.

6 You shouldn't working here so late.

7 I cant ring my boss now; he's already left.

8 Shall I give you a hand?

Use: Offers / polite requests

2 Put the words in the correct order to form offers/requests.

1 pick / I / Shall / up / later / you / ?

2 that, / you / Could / repeat / please / ?

3 here, / sit / May / I / please / ?

4 Jane, / to / I / Can / speak / please / ?

5 moment / interrupt / I / May / for / you / a / ?

6 order / I / Shall / a / taxi / ?

Use: Ability

3 Write four sentences about things you are/aren't able to do using *can/can't*. Use these ideas if you want.

● speak Chinese ● use Word ● drive a car ● ride a bike ● use PowerPoint
● play rugby ● chair meetings well ● give good presentations

Example: I can use Word, but I can't use PowerPoint.

Notice the different pronunciation of *can* /kæn/ and *can't* /kɑːnt/.

Use: Obligation / lack of obligation

4 Rewrite the sentences using *have to / don't/doesn't have to / must/mustn't*.

1 It is essential that visitors don't touch the exhibition.
Visitors ___mustn't touch the exhibition___ .

2 Is it necessary for you to work until 6 p.m.?
Do _____ ?

3 It isn't necessary for them to send the report off today.
They _____ .

4 It is essential that all staff sign in before 8 a.m.
All staff _____ .

5 Don't tell anyone about the new contract – it's a secret.
You _____ .

6 Don't forget to ask Maggie about the meeting.
You _____ .

Use: Permission   **5 Write sentences asking for permission to do the following.**

1 Start work later tomorrow
   May I start work later tomorrow, please?

2 Spend some money from your department's budget

3 Take a day off next week

4 Use a colleague's computer

5 Use your boss's office for a while

6 Take a short break

Use: Possibility   **6 Write five things you may/might (not) do over the following week using these phrases.**

- take a day off work   ● go to a football match   ● work on Saturday
- give a presentation   ● buy a new TV   ● have lunch out

Example: *I might take a day off work next week.*

Use: Advice   **7 Complete the sentences using *should/shouldn't*.**

1 It's very late. I think we ...
2 Sales are down, but I don't think we ...
3 That camera's on special offer. I think you ...
4 I'm fed up with my job. Do you think I ... ?
5 The train fares are quite expensive. I think we ...
6 I've seen a job ad for a marketing manager. Do you think I ... ?

Consolidation   **8 Choose the correct options.**

1 All the staff think you *shall / should* apply for the new manager job.
2 *May / Could* you send in the next candidate, please?
3 I *can't / mustn't* understand a thing Sharon is saying.
4 I can see you're busy. *Shall / Must* I give Pam a call for you?
5 Having a new CEO *must / may* help the situation here at work.
6 The company *shall / might* not invest in WEK any more.
7 Unfortunately, I *can't / couldn't* make last Tuesday's meeting.

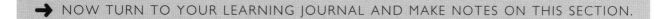

➔ NOW TURN TO YOUR LEARNING JOURNAL AND MAKE NOTES ON THIS SECTION.

Conditionals

 Before you do these exercises, look at page 58 of the Reference section.

Form: Conditionals

1 Match the sentence halves. Then decide whether each sentence uses conditional 1 or conditional 2.

1 We'll have to increase production ...

2 What would you do ...

3 If participants' feedback gets worse, ...

4 People wouldn't believe us if ...

5 If we don't find a buyer for the company soon, ...

6 I would change jobs ...

a ... we'll probably close down.

b ... if your company closed down?

c ... if sales increase further.

d ... we told them how bad things were.

e ... if I found a better one.

f ... we'll have to cancel the business programme.

Use: Conditional 1 – future possibilities

2 Choose the correct options.

1 If I still feel ill tomorrow, I *'ll stay / stay* at home.

2 If it *doesn't / won't* rain later on, I'll go for a walk during my lunch break.

3 I *might come / came* to the party, if you *don't / won't* mind.

4 Will you chair the meeting if Myra *will take / takes* the minutes?

5 I *'m not / won't be* surprised if I *won't / don't* get the job.

6 Bob *will help / helps* you with the report if you *ask / will ask* him.

> If the *if* clause comes first in the sentence, the intonation rises on it: *If you want to check, have a look in the manual.*

3 Complete the sentences using the correct form of the verbs in brackets.

1 If you _____ (be) late for work again, your line manager _____ (sack) you.

2 We _____ (go) without you if you _____ (not/hurry) up.

3 If we _____ (see) Jim, we _____ (give) him your message.

4 We _____ (stop) for a break if you _____ (be) tired.

5 If we _____ (not/leave) soon, we _____ (miss) the bus!

6 Business _____ (improve) if interest rates _____ (go) down.

7 If you _____ (not/read) the report carefully, you _____ (not/understand) it.

Use: Conditional 2 – imaginary future situations

4 Complete the sentences using the correct form of the verbs in brackets.

1 If I were younger, I _____ (study) foreign languages.

2 If the office wasn't so small, I _____ (put) another desk in.

3 I _____ (go) shopping if I _____ (have) more time.

4 If the company _____ (offer) Jack more money, he might stay on here.

5 He wouldn't get the job, even if he _____ (try).

6 We _____ (not/attend) the course if we _____ (not/enjoy) it.

7 More people _____ (shop) here if we _____ (reduce) our prices.

8 If I _____ (live) outside the city centre, I _____ (need) a car.

5 Complete the e-mail using the words in the box.

be	built	make	might	moved	would

Of course, if we [1]_____ a new factory in Lanchester, we [2]_____ definitely make huge savings. For example, land costs there would [3]_____ twice as cheap as here in Bilton. We also think that if we [4]_____ to Lanchester, the company might perhaps [5]_____ savings in terms of insurance costs. Also the cost of wages [6]_____ be lower.

6 Write sentences to say what you would do in these situations.

- you win $1m
- you lose your job
- the price of petrol rises substantially
- you fail your examinations
- you miss your bus to work
- you see someone steal in a shop

Example: If I won $1m, I'd buy a yacht.

Use: Conditional 2 – advice

7 Give advice using the ideas in the box.

buy new laptop	organize a social event	send out marketing flyers
speak to a manager	take on more staff	

1 A colleague wants to improve his computer equipment.
   If I was/were you, I'd buy a new laptop from Superdeals.
2 Your team needs advice for increasing sales.
3 Your colleague needs to deal with a bullying boss.
4 Your staff have to get a project back on schedule.
5 The team manager needs to improve morale.

Consolidation

8 Find and correct the errors in these sentences. Three of the sentences are correct.

1 If you will want help, Janet will assist you.
2 We'll go out for lunch if the weather gets better.
3 What would you do if your boss would make you redundant?
4 If all the staff will book flights together, they get a discount.
5 I come and see you later in the office if I have time.
6 If you rang the office, you probably wouldn't get an answer anyway.
7 You might enjoy yourself at the conference if you come.
8 If I would be you, I'd tell your boss about your concerns with the project.
9 We won't finish this report if we won't do it today.
10 We wouldn't come to the meeting even if you would invite us.

➡ NOW TURN TO YOUR LEARNING JOURNAL AND MAKE NOTES ON THIS SECTION.

–*ing* forms and infinitives

 Before you do these exercises, look at page 58 of the Reference section.

Form: –*ing* forms and infinitives

1 Match the sentence halves.

1 I'm afraid that smoking ...
2 Are you interested in ...
3 Have you decided ...
4 Please don't leave ...
5 The CEO expects staff ...
6 Did you have difficulties in ...

a ... without saying goodbye.
b ... filling in the forms?
c ... isn't permitted in the building.
d ... to work more and more hours.
e ... to change jobs?
f ... finding out more about the company?

Use: Verb + infinitive

| check | get | meet |
| pay | take | turn |

2 Complete the sentences using the correct form of the verbs in the box.

1 We decided _____ a taxi.
2 My boss agreed _____ for my business trip.
3 I forgot _____ off the machine when I went out.
4 Have you arranged _____ Merlin later on?
5 I offered _____ my colleague's e-mails while she was off sick.
6 I've managed _____ tickets to the opera for our clients.

Use: Verb + object + infinitive

This structure is used a lot in reported speech (see page 61).

3 Rewrite the sentences so that they mean the same.

1 'Could you please help me to finish this report?'
   My colleague asked me *if I could help him finish this report.*
2 'I hope you get the promotion.' My friend wanted me ...
3 'You mustn't tell anyone about the staff changes.' Our boss told us not ...
4 'There may be further redundancies next year.' We were warned to expect ...
5 'Don't forget to post that letter.' My colleague reminded me ...
6 'I told you that you shouldn't be late.' You were warned ...

Use: Adjective + infinitive

| bring | concentrate |
| do | see | sit |
| work |

4 Complete the sentences using the verbs in the box. Add *to* in the correct place.

1 You need to be determined _____ well.
2 It's too hot in this office _____ on anything.
3 Has it been interesting _____ on this project?
4 I was surprised _____ so many people at the event.
5 It's hard _____ in front of a screen all day.
6 How expensive was it _____ in the staff on overtime?

Use: Preposition + –ing form

about losing
at making
before going
in attending
of talking
on writing

5 Complete the sentences using the phrases in the box.

1 Are you interested _____ the conference?

2 I'm really tired _____ about this.

3 Are you worried _____ your job?

4 Please concentrate _____ the e-mail.

5 Jeremy is the best person _____ money.

6 Let's meet up in the canteen for lunch _____ to the meeting.

Use: Verb + –ing form

6 Use the prompts to write sentences.

1 you / enjoy / play / badminton / free time?

2 I / suggest / go / home

3 stop / make / that / noise

4 I / not / mind / work / late

5 we need / to keep / promote / product

6 you / finished / write / article?

Use: –ing forms as nouns (gerunds)

7 Put the words in the correct order to form sentences.

1 Spending / gone / has / goods / down / on / electrical

2 be / for / time / Making / appraisals / will / impossible

3 start / meeting / the / Waiting / for / to / was / boring

4 of / part / best / staff / managing / is / The / my / role

5 is / differences / cultural / Understanding / key / to / international / business

Consolidation

8 Complete the sentences using the correct form (–ing form or infinitive) of the verbs in brackets.

1 I promised _____ (give) my colleague a lift.

2 Don't you mind _____ (chair) meetings?

3 I dislike _____ (have) to work Saturdays.

4 My boss suggested _____ (hold) the product launch next week.

5 Have you finished _____ (write) your report?

6 I enjoy _____ (work) here.

7 My friend asked me _____ (help) her with her application.

8 I really hope _____ (go) to the United States one day.

9 Are you good at _____ (manage) staff?

10 (work) _____ at Electox is great.

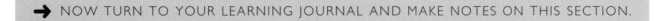

➔ NOW TURN TO YOUR LEARNING JOURNAL AND MAKE NOTES ON THIS SECTION.

Comparatives and superlatives

★ Before you do these exercises, look at page 59 of the Reference section.

Form: Comparatives and superlatives

1 Find and correct the errors in these sentences.

1 Is it easyer to take the train or drive?

2 Which is the more successful product out of these three?

3 Your TV is more moderner than mine.

4 This car is less efficient as my previous one.

5 Is your role the same than mine?

6 Our office is much biger now.

Use: Comparatives

2 Complete the sentences using the words in the box.

bit	expensive
further	more
nearer	than

1 The new office is _____ to my home than the previous one.

2 Taking a taxi would be quicker for you _____ waiting for a bus.

3 Please could you work a _____ faster, everyone?

4 The company cars are _____ economical than they used to be.

5 Is your new workplace much _____ away than your last one?

6 Buying a new car would be much more _____ than repairing this one.

3 Complete the sentences using the appropriate comparative form of the adjectives in bold.

1 Jacky's desk isn't very **big**. Mine is _____ .

2 My current job isn't **difficult**. Yours is _____ .

3 The sales assistants aren't very **helpful**. They used to be _____ .

4 I found the first session quite **interesting**, but I thought the second one was even _____ .

5 Gosh, this task is too **complicated**! Let's try one that's _____ .

Use: Superlatives

4 Complete the sentences using the appropriate superlative form of the adjectives in bold.

1 This office is very **old**. It's _____ in the whole building.

2 Mikka's a very **good** worker. He's _____ worker I know.

3 The IT suite here is **modern**. It's _____ suite the company has.

4 My line manager is so **funny**. He's _____ man I've ever met.

5 My desk is really **small**. I think it's _____ in the whole office.

6 The sales figures are **low**. They're _____ we've had in ages.

5 Put the words in the correct order to form sentences.

1 member / creative / the / Lema / is / least / staff / of

2 in / city / is / London / the / biggest / England

3 comprehensive / the / report / Your / is / most / read / I've

4 interesting / the / is / My / job / least / here

5 their / lowest / since / Sales / are / at / 1999

Use: Comparative and superlative of adverbs

6 Complete the sentences using comparative or superlative adverb form of the adjectives in brackets.

1 Between January and March, Forby's share price rose _____ than in the previous year. (sharp)

2 In this quarter, our share price dropped _____ than investors predicted. (quick)

3 Bolt's share price has increased much _____ than Profi's. (dramatic)

4 Of Priceextra, 100pc and Profi, Profi saw its share price fall _____ . (slow)

5 Shares in logistics companies are being sold cheaply, but those of mailing companies are being sold _____ . (cheap)

See the 'Word families' sections on pages 63 and 65 for help with the vocabulary in this exercise.

Use: Useful phrases

7 Rewrite the sentences so that they mean the same.

1 There are fewer staff at Compete than three years ago.
There aren't *as many staff at Compete as three years ago.*

2 The Xtra project is more important to us than the BriefU project.
The BriefU project is _____ .

3 The amount of time spent on paperwork is similar in our London and Berlin offices.
People in London spend about the same _____ .

4 Sally's computer is much more efficient than mine.
My computer isn't _____ .

5 Fewer people are taking part in training than ten years ago.
Not as _____ .

Consolidation

8 Complete the sentences using the correct form of the words in brackets.

1 My colleague speaks German _____ than I do. (good)

2 The project is not as _____ as I expected. (complicated)

3 You will all need to work _____ this year. (hard)

4 Who's your _____ salesperson this month? (bad)

5 We need to be _____ than we have been. (organized)

6 Mark is _____ PA we've ever had. (reliable)

7 Sales are not going as _____ as we hoped. (good)

➔ NOW TURN TO YOUR LEARNING JOURNAL AND MAKE NOTES ON THIS SECTION.

Relative clauses

★ Before you do these exercises, look at page 59 of the Reference section.

Form: Relative clauses

I Look at these sentences and decide whether each one:
a gives essential information
b gives non-essential, extra information
c could leave out the relative pronouns
d contains pronouns that could be replaced with *that*.

1 The man who has just left is the CEO.
2 I haven't managed to read the report that you wrote.
3 The work on the building, which only started in June, is already behind schedule.
4 An award will be given to the staff member whose sales are the highest.
5 Mikka Erkkinen, who has joined us from Helsinki, will be working in Finance.
6 Janet Staples, whose role has recently changed, isn't coming to today's meeting.
7 The man who just walked past is my boss.
8 The woman who you need to talk to is in Unit C2.

2 Add the missing commas to these sentences.

1 Joseph who lives in Birmingham works in the HR department.
2 Marian Cavender whose team is based in New York is taking early retirement.
3 Kris who runs the logistics department is thinking of setting up his own business.

Use: Defining clauses

3 Choose the correct options.

Dear Mr Wang

I am writing to apologize for the problems [1] *that / who* you had with the order [2] *that / what* you placed on 21 March (ref 30549).
It is likely that the staff member [3] *who / which* processed your order made a mistake when writing down the details [4] *whose / which* you gave them, although we cannot say for certain [5] *which / whose* fault it is.
Sam Coleson, [6] *that / who* is our Deliveries Manager, will call you asap to discuss a compensation package [7] *which / who* we hope will be acceptable to you.
I apologize again for any difficulties [8] *that / who* you may have.

Yours sincerely
Frances McCarthy

Use: Non-defining clauses

4 Combine the sentence pairs into one sentence using *who*, *which* or *whose*.

1 Madis is about 50 years old. Madis is our team leader.

   Madis, who is about 50 years old, is our team leader.

2 Britta comes from Sweden. Britta has just been made Production Manager.

3 The printer cost $1m. The printer has helped us to extend our business.

4 John's car has broken down. John has become Head of Department.

5 Our new software was expensive. Our new software has enabled us to improve our company's systems.

6 Nadja's colleague is off sick. Nadja is leading today's meeting.

7 The offices are very old. The offices are located in Coventry city centre.

8 Petra is often late for work. Petra is the lead organizer for the annual conference.

Use: Relative clauses

5 What is the difference in meaning between the sentences in each pair?

1 a The printer which we bought last month has already broken down twice.
  b The printer, which we bought last month, has already broken down twice.

2 a There are two staff members who are based in California.
  b There are two staff members, who are based in California.

6 In which of these sentences can the relative pronoun be left out?

1 The meeting, which is scheduled for 12 p.m., has been postponed.

2 The member of staff that made the suggestion was praised by management.

3 Do you know about the contracts which Siobhan is sorting out?

4 We haven't seen the e-mail that our colleague was speaking about.

5 I listened to the voicemail which you left me.

6 I haven't seen the woman who has been taken on in Accounts.

Consolidation

7 Find and correct the errors in the sentences. Three of the sentences are correct.

THE SHOP THAT SELLS THE STUFF THAT OTHER PEOPLE HAVE THAT MAKES YOU THINK I WONDER WHERE THEY GOT THAT?

www.CartoonStock.com

1 I've found out the names of those employees which will need to move offices.

2 I hope to move to an organization that has a better reputation than this one.

3 The fax to Thorns, that I should have sent yesterday, is still on my desk.

4 The exhibition, which will take place in June, is going to be held in Stuttgart.

5 The software which I ordered it hasn't arrived yet.

6 Joona who is our latest recruit used to work for GOAL.

7 Our regular receptionist, who is excellent by the way, is on leave today.

8 Jakob's the person which computer was found damaged.

→ NOW TURN TO YOUR LEARNING JOURNAL AND MAKE NOTES ON THIS SECTION.

Articles

★ Before you do these exercises, look at page 60 of the Reference section.

Form: A/an

1 Write *a* or *an* before the nouns.

1 ___ result   6 ___ pension scheme
2 ___ desk   7 ___ university
3 ___ hour   8 ___ event
4 ___ worker   9 ___ question
5 ___ engineer   10 ___ European

> The 'Word families' section on page 67 gives examples of jobs and professions – which are used with the indefinite article (*a/an*).

Use: A/an

2 Add *a*, *an* or *another* to the sentences where necessary.

1 We've launched new product.
2 My brother works as teacher.
3 Are you operator or receptionist?
4 It's very exciting project.
5 That was lovely cup of coffee. Can I have cup?

> See the 'Pronunciation' section on page 62 for tips on linking words such as *an* and *another*.

Form: The

3 Match the categories (1–8) with the examples (a–f). Then decide which examples are preceded by *the* and which have no article (–).

1 continent   a Alps
2 road   b *Daily Telegraph*
3 city   c Edinburgh
4 mountain range   d fire brigade
5 river   e Nile
6 emergency service   f South America
7 newspaper   g supper
8 meal   h Willow Terrace

Use: The

4 Find and correct the errors. Three of the sentences are correct.

1 Frankfurt Airport is in Germany.
2 Is your office in city centre?
3 I usually have breakfast at work these days.
4 My favourite programme, *Business Time*, is on radio tonight.
5 My uncle used to be in police.
6 Our company is biggest in the sector.
7 My line manager and I live in same street.
8 I'd like my computer to go on left of the desk.
9 What's time, please?
10 I've been working in the south-east of Scotland for three years.

Use: *A/an*, *the* **5 What is the difference in meaning between the sentences in each pair?**

1 a The CEO has just sacked the receptionist.
  b The CEO has just sacked a receptionist.

  Sentence (a) implies that there is only one receptionist.
  Sentence (b) implies that there is more than one.

2 a I found a mobile under the table.
  b I found the mobile under the table.

3 a Tara needs the new computer.
  b Tara needs a new computer.

4 a I love the music playing in reception.
  b I love music playing in reception.

5 a Jakob sat at a large table to do his work.
  b Jakob sat at the large table to do his work.

6 a Did you get a job in Madrid?
  b Did you get the job in Madrid?

Consolidation **6 Complete the sentences with *a/an*, *the* or no article (–).**

1 Oh dear, _____ sky's really dark.

2 I'm exhausted. I really need _____ holiday.

3 Is Estonian _____ hard language to learn?

4 What's _____ colour of your new office furniture?

5 _____ dinner's ready, everyone.

6 Please don't touch _____ wires. They're dangerous.

7 Have you seen our car? I'll clean _____ car tomorrow, I think.

8 Khalid is _____ most experienced operator.

9 _____ swimming is a popular activity among staff.

10 This is _____ best day of my life!

11 I stayed in _____ dirty hotel in the city last year.

12 Have you been to _____ bank yet?

13 You'd better hurry – we've only got half _____ hour for lunch.

14 I live in _____ north of Spain.

15 Have you ever been to _____ France?

16 _____ fruit and veg are good for you.

→ NOW TURN TO YOUR LEARNING JOURNAL AND MAKE NOTES ON THIS SECTION.

Determiners

★ Before you do these exercises, look at page 60 of the Reference section.

Form   **1 Put these words into the correct column.**

advice   employees   energy   euros   finance   information   leaflet   lorry
manager   marketing   offices   suggestion   warehouse

See the 'Spelling'
section on page 67 for
more on countable and
uncountable nouns.

countable singular	countable plural	uncountable

Use: *Some* and *any*   **2 Complete the sentences using *some* or *any*.**

1 There have been _____ applicants for the job already.

2 Haven't you sold _____ tickets yet?

3 I'd like _____ more information about your training courses, please.

4 Have you got _____ tea left?

5 I'm sorry, but I haven't got _____ money on me.

6 We haven't had _____ problems with the new software.

7 Please could you pass me _____ headed paper?

8 They haven't put _____ prices on these goods.

9 The IT department has ordered _____ new printers.

10 There hasn't been _____ interest in our new range.

Use: *(A) little* and   **3 What is the difference in meaning between the sentences in each pair?**
(a) few
1 a Few staff were at the meeting.
    b A few staff were at the meeting.

2 a I speak little English.
    b I speak a little English.

4 Complete the sentences using *(a) little* **or** *(a) few* **and the words in the box.**

hotels	milk	mistakes	people	petrol	reports
	suggestions	time	unemployment		

1 My PA's excellent at typing and makes very _____ _____ .

2 Yesterday, I had to write _____ _____ on behalf of my boss.

3 I'd like _____ _____ in my coffee, please.

4 I love it here. There are _____ _____ I'd rather stay in than this one.

5 Would you like _____ more _____ to help you?

6 There's _____ _____ in this region. We're so lucky.

7 Could you hurry up? We've got very _____ _____ .

8 We've got _____ _____ left, so I'm sure we'll get home.

9 We've had _____ good _____ today, so thank you for these.

Use: *Much, many,*
a lot of / lots of

5 Choose the correct options.

1 We haven't had *many / much* enquiries today.

2 Do you drink *much / many* coffee?

3 There are *much / a lot of* taxis outside the office.

4 I haven't got *much / many* time.

5 I eat *a lot of / much* fast food.

6 We saw *lots of / much* good practice in the company.

7 How *much / many* foreign languages do you speak?

8 There aren't *many / much* experienced staff here.

9 I've got *many / a lot of* envelopes if you need some.

10 People had *lots of / much* good ideas at the meeting.

Consolidation

6 Choose the correct options.

Dear Sally

How are things?

Is there [1] *any / many* more news about Dave leaving?

I've just got back from a business trip to Stuttgart. Unfortunately, [2] *a few /
few* irritating things happened. Firstly, I had [3] *some / any* trouble with the car
on the way to the airport. I had [4] *little / few* time before the flight, so I rushed
into one of the airport shops to buy [5] *some / any* magazines – and ended up
losing my wallet. Although [6] *a lot of / much* people joined in the search, we
couldn't find it, and with just [7] *a little / a few* minutes before the flight, I had
to go without it. Then I'd ordered [8] *some / any* food for the flight, but I didn't
get [9] *anything / something* at all, so I was starving by the time I arrived.
Finally, [10] *a few / a little* baggage handlers were off sick, so there were
[11] *some / any* delays at baggage reclaim.

→ NOW TURN TO YOUR LEARNING JOURNAL AND MAKE NOTES ON THIS SECTION.

Passives

 Before you do these exercises, look at page 61 of the Reference section.

Form

1 Which of the <u>underlined</u> verbs are passive?

See page 80 for some common irregular past participles.

> Online psychometric testing [1] <u>is being introduced</u> by a national charity in 2011. The company [2] <u>is adopting</u> the system to help it shortlist applicants for jobs. Such tests [3] <u>have been used</u> widely by international companies for over a decade, but [4] <u>have not been chosen</u> as often by voluntary organizations. 'Twenty potential candidates [5] <u>are asked</u> to complete the tests, after which five applicants [6] <u>are shortlisted</u>', said a spokesman. 'Psychometric tests can indicate a candidate's suitability to work in this field. So far, we [7] <u>have found</u> the system really helpful in our recruitment process.'

2 Find and correct the errors in these passive sentences.

1 A leading London accountant was elect to a senior post within the industry.

2 An established insurance firm, which locates to the north of Warsaw, has gone bankrupt.

3 MK Vehicles has taken over by its rivals.

4 It is expect that staff at R Media will receive a pay increase of 4%.

5 A project aimed at helping companies become more competitive have been launched by SMT Finance Group.

Use: Formal/impersonal

3 Which sentence in each pair is more formal? Which sentences use the passive?

1 a Employees are not required to do overtime.
  b We don't require employees to do overtime.

2 a Someone will deal with the complaints straight away.
  b The complaints will be dealt with straight away.

3 a All delegates are requested to check in between 9 and 11 a.m.
  b Please could all delegates check in between 9 and 11 a.m.?

4 a A decision was expected yesterday.
  b Everyone expected a decision yesterday.

Use: By

4 Use the prompts to write passive sentences, adding *by* where necessary.

Job titles often have initial capital letters (see also page 67).

1 meeting / cancel / last Tuesday / Regional Manager
<u>The meeting was cancelled last Tuesday by the Regional Manager.</u>

2 applicants / interview / next week / HR Manager

3 seminar / currently / organize / Training Director

4 presentation / give / yesterday / Jon

5 £1,000 / spend / already / on software / IT Assistant

6 eco-friendly taxi / might / develop / Coventry company / next two years

Use: Systems and processes

5 Complete the description of a recruitment process using the words in the box.

are	been	given	have	is	sent	will

All new jobs [1] _____ advertised in the local paper. Applicants are [2] _____ a comprehensive application pack in the post. Once completed forms have [3] _____ received, a meeting is arranged to shortlist candidates and to decide when interviews [4] _____ be held. Letters are then sent out to shortlisted applicants, inviting them to an interview led by the HR Director. After the interviews [5] _____ been arranged and have taken place, the successful candidate [6] _____ sent a letter offering him/her the position. All unsuccessful candidates are [7] _____ feedback on their application and interview.

Use: Emphasizing an action

6 Rewrite the sentences so that they mean the same.

1 The company has promoted two members of staff.

Two members of staff _____ .

2 Someone else will sign off the invoices while Jack is on leave.

While Jack is on leave, the invoices _____ .

3 The organization launched the new *Inspire me* DVD yesterday.

The new *Inspire me* DVD _____ .

4 People send in their timesheets to Finance every Friday.

Every Friday, timesheets _____ .

Consolidation

7 Find and correct the errors in the passive sentences in the article.

Exhibitors from around the world have invited to take part in the country's largest flooring trade show. Over 140 firms have already booked space at the Big Floor Fair, which being organized by Erkki OY. The three-day event will bring together importers, exporters, manufacturers and wholesalers. Show spokesman Peter Laing said: 'Last year's show attended by over 1,000 delegates – but I think that record will be broke this year! An advert for the show placed in a national newspaper three weeks ago, and we have already received twice as many enquiries as this time last year.'

➜ NOW TURN TO YOUR LEARNING JOURNAL AND MAKE NOTES ON THIS SECTION.

Reported speech

 Before you do these exercises, look at page 61 of the Reference section.

Form: Reported speech

1 Match the sentence halves.

1 We asked all our colleagues ...   a ... ignore rumours of redundancies.

2 Ann said not to ...   b ... to help us with deliveries, as we were so busy.

3 Mark told his team to ...   c ... apply for promotion, as she was so talented.

4 I advised my colleague to ...   d ... want to do any more overtime.

5 Staff said they didn't ...   e ... wait for her if she was late for the meeting.

Use: Tense change

2 Rewrite the sentences as reported speech using past tenses.

1 'Staff morale isn't very good.' Markus said ...

2 'Job losses are highly likely.' Benjamin said ...

3 'I've finished all my tasks.' I told my boss I ...

4 'I can't attend the team meeting.' Jacky said she ...

5 'Sales will rise over the next three months.' My boss said ...

6 'The photocopier doesn't work.' Carole said ...

7 'I don't like working weekends.' She said she ...

8 'We don't know why the office is so cold.' We said we ...

> For more on past tenses, see pages 10–11 and page 61.

Use: –ing form

3 Rewrite the sentences as reported speech.

1 'I didn't want Jenny to resign.' He denied ...

2 'Why don't we travel to the conference together?' My colleague suggested ...

3 'I think the May Hotel is the best place to stay.' My boss recommended ...

4 'We went to a good conference in Milan last year.' Sheila mentioned ...

5 'I've found a few problems with the budget.' Gerard reported ...

6 'I'm afraid it was me that switched off the machine.' The new operative admitted ...

Use: Infinitive

4 Rewrite the sentences as reported speech using the verbs in the box.

agree	decide
offer	promise
refuse	want

1 'No, I'm not going to write the report for you.' My assistant ...

2 'I could give you a lift to the station.' A colleague ...

3 'Oh, if you really want me to, I'll give the presentation next month.' Cecile ...

4 'I'll definitely finish the summary by Friday.' My boss ...

5 'We're finally made up our minds. We're going to leave.' Two staff members ...

6 'I'd like you to arrange a meeting next week.' My boss ...

Use: Objective and infinitive

advised   ask   give
me   to cancel
to do   you

5 Complete the dialogue using the words in the box.

Marie: So what did Horst want to see you about yesterday?

Joachim: Oh, he just asked me to [1] _____ the opening talk at the conference in Bilbao. I was a bit surprised. I expected him to [2] _____ Joanne, as she's got more experience.

Marie: I see – did you say yes?

Joachim: At first I said no, but he [3] _____ me to reconsider.

Marie: You mean he actually warned [4] _____ not to disagree with him?

Joachim: It wasn't exactly a warning, but I felt he was telling me [5] _____ what he wanted. Anyway, after a long silence, I agreed. He then invited [6] _____ to go and see him tomorrow, so we can prepare the talk together.

Marie: That sounds good.

Joachim: Hmm, I suppose so, although I've got to fly out on Monday already. Martin reminded me [7] _____ all the appointments I've got next week.

Marie: Well, I'd better let you get on. Good luck!

Use: Time phrases

6 Add the correct time phrases to the reported speech.

1 'I'm starting the review tomorrow.'

She said she was starting the review _____ .

2 'I went to Japan on business two years ago.'

She said she went to Japan on business two years _____ .

3 'The staff are all in a meeting now.'

He said the staff were all in a meeting _____ .

4 'You didn't sell enough stock yesterday.'

She said I didn't sell enough stock _____ .

Consolidation

7 Read the voicemail message, then complete the e-mail below reporting what Carolyn has told you.

So, while I'm away, please could you check my e-mails? Please could you also open any post addressed to me? Oh yes, don't forget to deal promptly with any orders. It might be a good idea to get some help from Sam. I don't want a big pile of invoices to do when I get back, so please could you process the invoices as they come in? I think there will also be a few bills to deal with. I don't know exactly when I'll be back, but it will probably be ...

Hi Sam

I've just heard from Carolyn about covering her leave. She asked me

[1] _____ . She also asked [2] _____ .

She reminded me [3] _____ . She recommended [4] _____ . Carolyn

said she [5] _____ lots of invoices to do and asked [6] _____ . She also

said she [7] _____ . She told me that she [8] _____ .

→ NOW TURN TO YOUR LEARNING JOURNAL AND MAKE NOTES ON THIS SECTION.

Companies and offices

★ Before you do these exercises, look at page 62 of the Reference section.

Meaning

1 Choose the correct options.

1 Although the training organization TrainULike only set up business last year, it is doing well. It is *expanding / increasing* into new markets.

2 The renowned electronics firm DigiKom has a good reputation. It is *recognized / seen* internationally.

3 The Chairman of the upcoming new company wanted to establish a solid client *base / basis* before moving into new areas.

4 When choosing a new job, a clean *environment / economy* is important to many people.

5 When the contractor came into the office, he worked at the *hot / limited* desk.

6 Despite reports in the press of a hostile takeover, the two companies had in fact decided to work together and had *merged / partnered*.

Spelling

2 Complete the missing words.

1 Last year, GlobalTrain, a large training company, t _ _ _ o _ _ _ LearnLocal, a small company based in south-west England.

2 Have you heard that PG Trips and FunHols are m _ _ _ _ _ _ ? They hope to have a stronger presence on the holiday market by working together.

3 Because of our successful marketing strategy and the innovative results from research and development, we are now i n t _ _ _ _ _ _ _ _ _ _ _ _ _ r e c _ _ _ _ _ _ _ _ .

4 To remain c o _ _ _ _ _ _ _ _ _ , we need to reduce our prices and deliver more quickly.

5 After the scandal surrounding the members of the Board, the company's r e p _ _ _ _ _ _ _ went downhill.

6 To gain access to the company premises, you need to show your s e _ _ _ _ _ _ pass at the gate.

Pronunciation

3 Mark the sounds that run together between separate words in the phrases below. Not all the phrases have sounds that run together.

1 We have to close offices in the regions.

2 A good reputation requires hard work.

3 RJ Chemicals is recognized internationally.

4 Take the lift to the third floor.

5 The takeover resulted in job losses.

6 A clean and friendly working environment is important to me.

7 We work solely with well-known companies.

8 We support upcoming companies in their development.

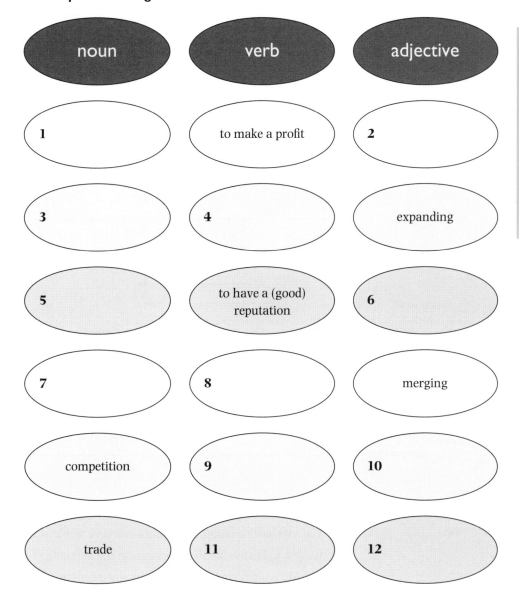

Collocations   **4 Which words can go in front of *company* and *office*?**

_____ company

_____ office

Word families   **5 Complete the diagram.**

noun	verb	adjective
1	to make a profit	2
3	4	expanding
5	to have a (good) reputation	6
7	8	merging
competition	9	10
trade	11	12

VOCABULARY PRACTICE

Consolidation   **6 Think of vocabulary relating to companies and offices that you might need to understand and/or use.**

1 Note it down.

2 Put it into sentences that you are likely to come across.

3 Practise saying and writing them.

➔ NOW TURN TO YOUR LEARNING JOURNAL AND MAKE NOTES ON THIS SECTION.

Finance

★ Before you do these exercises, look at page 63 of the Reference section.

Meaning **1 Label the sales graph using the correct phrases from the box.**

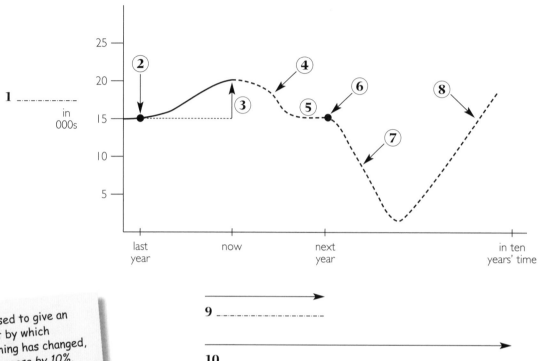

By is used to give an amount by which something has changed, e.g. *increase by 10%, fall by 5%.* To is used to give the actual figure, e.g. *increase to 20,000, fall to 300.* At is used to give a stable figure, e.g. *even out at £6,000.*

9 _____

10 _____

| exact figure (at past point) long-term outlook rough figure (at future point) |
| short-term outlook to be up by 30% to drop to even out |
| to nose-dive to rocket total sales figures |

Spelling **2 Choose the correct options.**

1 The *economic / economical* climate is not very stable at the moment.

2 We can't plan too far ahead because of the *unstability / instability* of the markets.

3 Nobody is interested in that product any more – it's become completely *inprofitable / unprofitable*.

4 Prices have plummeted. It is difficult to *preduce / predict* whether they will pick up again soon or not.

5 What's the *financial / financal* forecast?

6 Interest *rates / reats* have finally evened out.

7 The Finance Director was convinced that the *investation / investment* in new machinery would bring long-term benefits.

8 Following the takeover, *shear / share* prices dropped dramatically.

VOCABULARY PRACTICE

Pronunciation

3 **Look at the letter o in bold in these words. Write the words in the correct column of the table.**

board meeting   dr**o**p   f**o**recast   f**o**resee   l**oa**ns   n**o**se-dive   **o**verheads   pr**o**fit

r**o**cket   t**o**tal sales figures

/ɒ/ as in c**o**st	/əʊ/ as in **o**verdraft	/ɔː/ as in sh**o**rtage

Collocations

4 **Which words can go in front of *figures*? Write as many verbs, nouns or adjectives as you can.**

_____

_____   figures

_____

Word families

5 **Complete the table.**

For examples of some of these words in context, see Exercise 6 on page 21.

verb	noun
to rise	1
2	an increase
3	a drop
to fall	4
5	a decrease
to nose-dive	6

Consolidation

6 **Think of vocabulary relating to finance that you might need to understand and/or use.**

1 Note it down.

2 Put it into sentences that you are likely to come across.

3 Practise saying and writing them.

→ NOW TURN TO YOUR LEARNING JOURNAL AND MAKE NOTES ON THIS SECTION.

Human resources

★ Before you do these exercises, look at page 64 of the Reference section.

Meaning

1 Match the definitions (1–6) with the words/phrases (a–f).

1 someone who goes for a job interview
2 to send your CV to a potential new employer
3 to take on new members of staff
4 offering training to employees
5 a way of contributing to money received later in life
6 to tell your company you are leaving

a to apply for a job
b a candidate
c a pension scheme
d to give notice
e to recruit
f staff development

Spelling

2 Unjumble the words and phrases.

1 boj palntapicio   j _ _ a _ _ _ _ _ _ _ _ _ _ _
2 episarpea   a _ _ _ _ _ _ _ _
3 yomplere   e _ _ _ _ _ _ _
4 yncdndreua   r _ _ _ _ _ _ _ _ _
5 nnpioes   p _ _ _ _ _ _
6 mpdveotleen   d _ _ _ _ _ _ _ _ _ _

Pronunciation

3 Put the words in the correct column of the table, according to their stress pattern.

~~application~~   apply   recruitment   recruit   appraisal   appraisee   employer   employee   employ   salary   company   notice

ooOo	oO	oOo	ooO	Ooo	Oo
application					

Collocations   **4 Complete the sentences.**

1 My company is trying to speed up its _____ process so we can fill _____ posts with as little delay as possible.

2 Alex isn't in the office today. He went to the doctor's yesterday and has been signed off on _____ _____ for a week.

3 Many employees are joining the _____ at the moment due to the restructuring of the _____ , which is putting some jobs at risk.

4 The marketing department is expanding. It is taking on more _____ to work on the TV campaigns.

5 Our members of staff need to improve their presentation _____ , so we are offering _____ .

6 Tim believes he has enough managerial experience, so he intends to _____ for the Project Manager post that HR is currently _____ on the intranet at work.

For more on the use of the present continuous, see page 56.

Word families   **5 Complete the table.**

noun	verb	adjective
1	to apply for	2
redundancy		3
4	to employ	7
5		
6		
8	9	recruitable
appraisal	10	
(staff) development	11	

Consolidation   **6 Think of vocabulary relating to human resources that you might need to understand and/or use.**

1 Note it down.

2 Put it into sentences that you are likely to come across.

3 Practise saying and writing them.

IT'S THE NEW MANAGEMENT STRUCTURE, THE WORKER'S THE ONE AT THE BOTTOM...

FRAN

www.CartoonStock.com

➡ NOW TURN TO YOUR LEARNING JOURNAL AND MAKE NOTES ON THIS SECTION.

Logistics

★ Before you do these exercises, look at page 65 of the Reference section.

Meaning   **1 Complete the diagram using the words in the box.**

| batch | by rail | consignment | freight | in stock | in the warehouse | invoice |
| to mail out | to pay in instalments | to order | to dispatch | unit price |

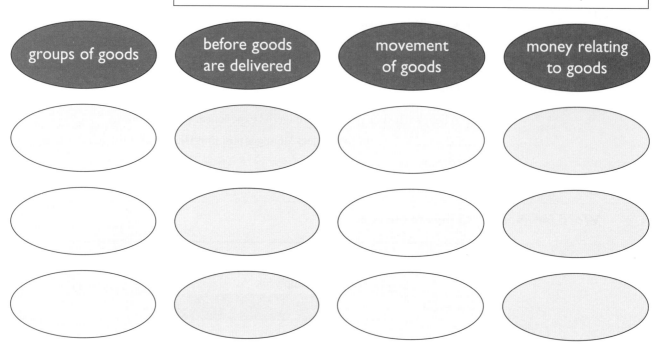

groups of goods   before goods are delivered   movement of goods   money relating to goods

Spelling   **2 Choose the correct options.**

1 The last *consinement / consignment* was damaged when it was delivered.

2 Due to increasing *freight / fright* costs, it is difficult to remain competitive.

3 Can you please send the *invoice / invoise* by the end of the week, as we are reaching our year end?

4 Your options are to pay in three *instalments / unstalments* or in full.

5 Crawford & Sons *supplyed / supplied* the electrical components on time.

6 We need to check all *deliveries / deliverys* before signing for them, in case they are damaged and we can't claim compensation later.

Pronunciation   **3** **Think about the pronunciation of the letters in bold in the following words. Tick the correct column.**

	/tʃ/ as in _**ch**air_	/ʃ/ as in _**sh**op_
shipment	☐	☐
dispat**ch**	☐	☐
pur**ch**ase	☐	☐
confirma**t**ion	☐	☐
bat**ch**	☐	☐
in**s**urance	☐	☐
finan**c**ial	☐	☐
check	☐	☐

Collocations   **4** **Which words and phrases can go with the noun _transport_ and the verb _to transport_?**

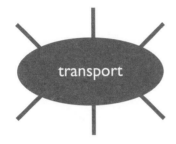

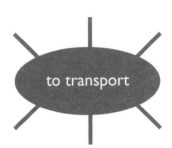

Word families   **5** **Write the corresponding adverbs for these adjectives.**

1 careful

2 considerate

3 direct

4 fast

5 immediate

6 slow

7 speedy

8 swift

For more on adjectives and adverbs, see page 59.

Consolidation   **6** **Think of vocabulary relating to logistics that you might need to understand and/or use.**

1 Note it down.

2 Put it into sentences that you are likely to come across.

3 Practise saying and writing them.

➡ NOW TURN TO YOUR LEARNING JOURNAL AND MAKE NOTES ON THIS SECTION.

Meetings and conferences

★ Before you do these exercises, look at page 66 of the Reference section.

Meaning

1 Match these words (1–4) with their synonyms (a–d).

1 to participate in a meeting   a a graph
2 to organize   b to arrange
3 an attendee   c to attend a meeting
4 a visual   d a participant

2 Match these words (1–6) with their antonyms (opposites) (a–f).

1 to hold a meeting   a to disagree
2 to pass round handouts   b to cancel the venue
3 to reach an agreement   c to cancel a meeting
4 to book the room   d a failure
5 a successful event   e to collect in (completed) forms
6 to attend a conference   f to miss an event

Spelling

3 Unjumble the words.

1 n t t p p o a i e m n   a _ _ _ _ _ _ _ _ _ _
2 s o n n q u r e i a e i t   q _ _ _ _ _ _ _ _ _ _ _ _
3 t n m s u i e   m _ _ _ _ _ _
4 t t e e n g o a i   n _ _ _ _ _ _ _ _
5 o o p o h t c p y   p _ _ _ _ _ _ _ _
6 e e e o o e i v d c n f r n c v _ _ _ _ _ _ _ _ _ _ _ _ _

Pronunciation

4 Mark the /ə/ sound in these words and phrases. There may be more than one in some words.

1 presenter
2 organize
3 cancel
4 write up a report
5 agree
6 book a venue
7 projector
8 attendance

Collocations **5 Complete the phrases using the verbs in the box. There may be more than one possible answer.**

| arrange | attend | book | cancel | fill in | hold | make | postpone |
| reach | take | write up |

1 _____ an agreement / a conclusion

2 _____ a form / a questionnaire

3 _____ a report / the minutes

4 _____ a room / a venue

5 _____ the minutes / notes

6 _____ a meeting / a conference / an event

7 _____ an appointment / a booking

8 _____ a suggestion / a proposal / an offer

Word families **6 Choose the correct noun that relates to each of the verbs in bold.**

1 **to disagree**   disagree / disagreeing / disagreement

2 **to postpone**   postpone / postponement / postponant

3 **to attend**   attendment / attendance / attend

4 **to organize**   organizal / organization / organizement

5 **to present**   presentation / presentment / presention

6 **to negotiate**   negotiator / negotiater / negotiatator

7 **to book**   book / booking / bookment

8 **to participate**   participal / participant / participer

9 **to discuss**   discuss / discussment / discussion

10 **to speak**   speakor / speaker / speakal

Consolidation **7 Think of vocabulary relating to meetings and conferences that you might need to understand and/or use.**

1 Note it down.

2 Put it into sentences that you are likely to come across.

3 Practise saying and writing them.

THE PURPOSE OF THIS MEETING IS FINDING SOMEONE WHO WILL TAKE THE BLAME FOR MY BAD DECISIONS.

PIERO TONIN

www.CartoonStock.com

➜ NOW TURN TO YOUR LEARNING JOURNAL AND MAKE NOTES ON THIS SECTION.

People and places

⭐ Before you do these exercises, look at page 67 of the Reference section.

Meaning   **1 Match these words (1–5) with their synonyms (a–e).**

1 head of buying   a co-worker

2 colleague   b shop floor

3 team leader   c premises

4 factory   d chief buyer

5 offices   e team manager

2 Match these words (1–5) with their antonyms (opposites) (a–e).

1 subordinate   a boss

2 partner   b city-centre location

3 on the outskirts   c on an industrial estate

4 easily accessible   d employee

5 in the countryside   e out of the way

Spelling   **3 Complete the missing words.**

1 The offices were on a hill o v _ _ _ _ _ _ _ _ _ a river.

2 The h _ _ _ office was in the city centre, but the distribution centre was on the
  o u _ _ _ _ _ _ _ .

3 The warehouse wasn't in a pretty l o _ _ _ _ _ _ , but it was near the motorway,
  so a c _ _ _ _ was good.

4 The international company was b _ _ _ _ i _ most countries in South America,
  as well as Europe and Japan.

5 The team manager delegated the job to his s u _ _ _ _ _ _ _ _ _ _ .

6 I work with a team of five people. We get on very well. Not everyone is lucky enough
  to have good c o _ _ _ _ _ _ _ _ .

7 He bought 50% of the company's shares and became a p a _ _ _ _ _ .

8 We were lucky to find such a good s e _ _ _ _ _ _ _ ; she is very efficient at
  organizing our meetings and typing up the minutes.

Pronunciation 4 **Look at the letter _a_ in bold in these words. Write the words in the correct column of the table.**

assistant   based in   centr**a**l   f**a**ctory   industri**a**l est**a**te   loc**a**tion   m**a**nager

p**a**rtner   s**a**les manager   subordin**a**te   w**a**rehouse

/eɪ/ as in p**ay**	/eə/ as in trade f**air**	/æ/ as in manuf**a**cture	/ɑː/ as in f**a**rther	/ə/ as in **a**ttend

Collocations 5 **Use the nouns and adjectives in the boxes below to complete these phrases. Some can be used more than once.**

1 _____ centre

2 _____ location

3 _____ manager

4 head of _____

Nouns

call   development   distribution   finance   sales   team   training

Adjectives

central   easily accessible   financial   industrial   pretty   rural

Word families 6 **Write the professions relating to these verbs and nouns.**

Remember to use an article before a job or profession (see page 60).

1 to manage   4 to manage selling   7 science

2 to buy   5 law   8 economy

3 to assist   6 to train   9 engineering

Consolidation 7 **Think of vocabulary relating to people and places that you might need to understand and/or use.**

1 Note it down.

2 Put it into sentences that you are likely to come across.

3 Practise saying and writing them.

➡ NOW TURN TO YOUR LEARNING JOURNAL AND MAKE NOTES ON THIS SECTION.

Planning

 Before you do these exercises, look at page 65 of the Reference section.

Meaning **1 Complete the crossword.**

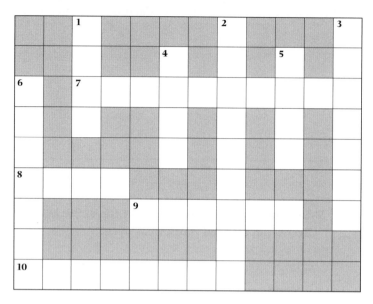

Down

1 when you think about the future and decide what to do

2 When companies move into new or different areas of business, they _____ .

3 to forecast the future, to say what you think will happen

4 something that may have a negative impact on your future success

5 When you think you can do something, you feel _____ to do it.

6 specific goals you set for the future

Across

7 targets or goals that are realistic and can be achieved

8 a plan or target

9 the way you see things to be in the future, the whole picture

10 a plan for success, the way forward

For more on referring to the future using *will* and *going to*, see page 57.

Spelling **2 Complete the sentences using the words in brackets in the correct form.**

1 Our Head of Planning is currently _____ (analyze) the data so she can set realistic targets.

2 Last year, JK Roberts _____ (diversify) into mobile technologies.

3 We need to have at least five good _____ (strategy) in place, so we can prove to Head Office that we are aware of future challenges.

4 They can't decide on a final plan. Since our meeting two months ago, they have _____ (draw up) three different versions.

5 The present reduction in the number of orders is _____ (enable) us to focus on improving processes.

6 Because the CEO needed figures last month, Alex has already _____ (set) targets for next year.

Pronunciation **3 Think about the pronunciation of the letter *r* in bold in these words. Tick the correct column.**

	pronounced /r/	not pronounced
risk	☐	☐
fo**r**ecast	☐	☐
cu**rr**ently	☐	☐
p**r**edict	☐	☐
realistic	☐	☐
dive**r**sify	☐	☐
failu**r**e	☐	☐
conce**r**n	☐	☐

Collocations **4 Look at the collocations in *italics*. Which are correct? Correct the incorrect ones.**

1 We need to *draw strategies*.

2 Long-term *plans were shown up* at the last Board meeting.

3 Either you *accept the risks* or you come up with new ideas.

4 David is working with an external agency to *do targets* for the whole department.

5 Before going any further, let's *assess the risks* involved in this project.

6 I'm only interested in hearing about *achieve goals*, not unrealistic ones.

Word families **5 Choose the correct options.**

1 They *cautious / cautiously* set targets for the next year.

For more on adverbs and adjectives, see page 59.

2 We can't wait any longer – we need an *immediately / immediate* decision.

3 I am confident that we have agreed *realistic / realistically* goals.

4 Don't you think those targets are *unrealistic / unrealistically*?

5 Our CEO speaks very *optimistic / optimistically* about the future, which is good.

6 The sales team is extremely *ambitiously / ambitious* and hard-working.

Consolidation **6 Think of vocabulary relating to planning and the future that you might need to understand and/or use.**

1 Note it down.

2 Put it into sentences that you are likely to come across.

3 Practise saying and writing them.

→ NOW TURN TO YOUR LEARNING JOURNAL AND MAKE NOTES ON THIS SECTION.

Production and processes

 Before you do these exercises, look at page 69 of the Reference section.

Meaning **1 Complete the crossword.**

		1		2		3
	4					
5						
6						
		7				
	8					

For more on passives, see page 61.

Down

1 'To work _____' means when workers in a factory work set hours around the clock.

2 a company or person who provides materials or services so that production can take place

3 Before a new product is launched, it is useful to _____ it.

5 Items that are produced are often costed per _____ .

7 These initials stand for 'quality assurance'.

Across

4 Production often needs to meet a deadline, and so runs to _____ .

6 to put new machinery in place

8 when a sample batch of new products is released on the market (5, 3)

Spelling **2 Correct the spelling mistakes in the words in *italics*.**

1 The company *implimented* a new health and safety *proceedure*.

2 The order was delivered in *consinements*.

3 Because of the large order, the *produktion* line had to work through the night.

4 The staff worked hard to keep to *shedule*.

5 RS Engineering changed *supplyer* because *deleivery* times were too long.

6 The technical testing team checks the *qualities* of the goods, as well as making sure they work.

7 We try to keep storage costs down by not having too much in *stoke*.

8 The forklift truck has broken down three times in the last year. We need to do more regular *maintenances* on it to try and avoid this happening again.

9 We have invested a lot of money in quality *asurance*, so we expect a high-quality end product.

Pronunciation

3 Mark the main stressed syllable in these words.

1 a process

2 to install

3 installation

4 a product

5 to produce

6 a warehouse

Collocations

4 Match the sentence halves.

1 When a new customer put in ...

2 Staff at Brown Chemicals have regular training so they know how to follow ...

3 Logiline has had to put up its prices due to the increase in ...

4 Companies that store less in ...

5 We do regular testing so we can assure ...

a ... health and safety procedures.

b ... a bulk order, RS Engineering had to take on extra staff.

c ... the warehouse can get more on the shop shelves and sell more.

d ... the highest quality of our products.

e ... transport costs by 20% over the last five years.

Word families

5 Write the corresponding verbs for these nouns.

1 process   to process

2 maintenance

3 update

4 schedule

5 product/production

6 purchase/purchasing

7 supplies/supplier

8 delivery

Consolidation

6 Think of vocabulary relating to production and processes that you might need to understand and/or use.

1 Note it down.

2 Put it into sentences that you are likely to come across.

3 Practise saying and writing them.

➜ NOW TURN TO YOUR LEARNING JOURNAL AND MAKE NOTES ON THIS SECTION.

Projects and teams

 Before you do these exercises, look at page 70 of the Reference section.

For more on -ing forms and infinitives, see page 58.

VOCABULARY PRACTICE

Meaning | **1 Choose the best option (a or b) to replace the words in *italics*.**

1 Rupert is good at keeping projects on track, so he's been appointed as *project manager*.
  a project leader   **b** project control

2 Although Hugo retires at the end of the month, he wants to *take the project to the end*, which is in three months' time.
  a conclude the project   **b** see the project through

3 Before the project starts, we need to clarify the customer's *requirements*.
  a specifications   **b** necessaries

4 I'm afraid the contractor has *quoted too low a price*. The actual costs will be higher.
  a underestimated   **b** quoted below

5 The project manager provided the team with the *timeframe* for the work they were about to start.
  a schedule   **b** calendar

6 Sasha was brought into the team because of her excellent IT *knowledge*.
  a talent   **b** skills

Spelling | **2 Complete the missing words.**

1 How much time have we got? What's the s _ _ _ _ u l e ?

2 Can you explain to Pete what he needs to do? I haven't got time to b _ _ _ f him.

3 Now our lorry is repaired, we can deliver the c _ _ s i _ _ _ _ n t.

4 What? Work can't start yet? Why have we got to p _ _ _ p _ _ _ the project?

5 Our customer's not happy with the design – we need to make some m _ d _ f _ c _ _ _ _ n s.

6 Tommy is going to be off sick for a few weeks, so we need to r e o r _ _ _ _ z e the team.

Pronunciation | **3 Put these words in the correct column of the table, according to their stress pattern.**

customer   developments   modifications   postpone   progress   project
reorganize   requirements   schedule   specifications

Oo	oO	oOo	Ooo	oOoo	oooOo
			customer		

4 Two of the words in Exercise 3 belong in two categories. Which words are they, and why?

Collocations

5 Complete the phrases in _italics_ using the verbs in the box.

confirm	delay	deliver	make	sign	work with

1 I'm afraid we've not been granted planning permission yet. We'll have to _____ _the start date_.

2 None of the team members has foreign language skills, so they are planning to _____ _people_ from a translation agency when they start the project in Europe.

3 That's the absolute latest the project has to be completed, so yes, I can _____ _the deadline_.

4 John had negotiated well, and he and the supplier reached agreement. They were both hoping to _____ _the contract_ as soon as possible.

5 During the team meeting, the project manager was careful to _____ _notes_ so that she had a record of the discussion in case any problems arose later.

6 We always aim to _____ _a consignment_ within 14 days of the order being placed.

Word families

6 Rewrite these nouns and noun phrases using a verb or verb phrase.

1 project proposal   to propose a project
2 project leader
3 reorganization of the team
4 confirmation of a deadline
5 schedule
6 modification
7 specification
8 estimation of costs
9 delay

Consolidation

7 Think of vocabulary relating to projects and teams that you might need to understand and/or use.

1 Note it down.
2 Put it into sentences that you are likely to come across.
3 Practise saying and writing them.

© Mike Baldwin / Cornered

www.CartoonStock.com

Being a team player is a good thing, until the project goes horribly wrong.

➡ NOW TURN TO YOUR LEARNING JOURNAL AND MAKE NOTES ON THIS SECTION.

Sales and marketing

 Before you do these exercises, look at page 71 of the Reference section.

Meaning   **1 Match these phrases (1–6) with their definitions (a–f).**

1 to advertise

2 to appeal to

3 cold-calling

4 a competitor

5 a potential customer

6 promotional materials

a to promote a product or service in such a way so as to encourage people to buy it

b materials such as brochures or websites used to promote items

c a possible new customer

d another company offering similar services or selling similar products to your own

e to attract, to be liked by

f when a salesperson phones a potential customer without prior arrangement

Spelling   **2 Look at the words in *italics* in the sentences below. Rewrite them according to the instructions in brackets.**

US/UK	=	change the spelling to the American/British spelling
plural	=	change the word to the plural
present/past tense	=	change the verb to the tense indicated

For more on past tenses, see page 56.

1 We *organised* the sales conference in a very short space of time. (US)

2 The Sales Department had *an enquiry* which could lead to a huge contract. (plural)

3 Johann *set up* the stand at the Frankfurt trade fair. (present tense)

4 Have you had many potential customers *enquiring* about your services following the publicity campaign? (UK)

5 Mario is the top sales representative in Europe. He *sells* over half a million units per quarter. (past tense)

6 Is it ethical to *publicize* new medicines before they've been fully tested? (UK)

Pronunciation   **3 Mark the sounds that run together in these sentences.**

1 His job is to look into attracting new customers.

2 Head Office has decided to set up a new distribution centre.

3 It is good practice to follow up cold calls with written confirmation.

4 Why not take out an advert to promote sales?

5 You could sell on the Internet.

6 We hope to move into markets overseas.

Collocations

4 Choose the correct options.

1 Our regional sales rep *followed up* / *moved up* the enquiry with a quote via e-mail.

2 I usually *attract* / *attend* the trade fair in San Francisco.

3 They're hoping to *market* / *shop* their products in South America as well as in the USA.

4 By the end of the negotiation, they still weren't able to *incline* / *agree* payment terms.

5 A huge amount of money was invested in *firing* / *launching* the advertising campaign.

6 The Marketing Department really needs to *promote* / *quote* the new products better, as sales have been very slow.

Word families

5 Look at the verbs in the box below and answer these questions.

1 What is the equivalent noun for each verb?

2 Which of the words have more than one possible spelling?

3 Which nouns have no plural?

to distribute	to enquire	to launch	to pay	to promote
	to publicize	to sell		

Consolidation

6 Think of vocabulary relating to sales and marketing that you might need to understand and/or use.

1 Note it down.

2 Put it into sentences that you are likely to come across.

3 Practise saying and writing them.

www.CartoonStock.com

→ NOW TURN TO YOUR LEARNING JOURNAL AND MAKE NOTES ON THIS SECTION.

Telephoning and e-mailing

★ Before you do these exercises, look at page 72 of the Reference section.

For more on modals, see page 57.

Meaning

1 Complete the definitions.

1 When you make a phone call and you manage to speak to the person, you g_____ th_____ .

2 When you make a phone call but don't manage to speak to the person, you may l_____ a m_____ on their a_____ or on their v_____ .

3 Sometimes when using a mobile phone, you might get c_____ o_____ if reception isn't very good.

4 If you have a document to send to your business associate, you can send it in an e-mail a_____ .

5 If an e-mail would be useful for someone else to see, you can f_____ it on to that person.

6 However, if the content of the e-mail is c_____ , then you need to think carefully about who you send it to.

7 I need to see the Sales Manager. Can you call her to make an a_____ , please?

8 I'm sorry you've had so many problems. Please put your c_____ in writing, and we will look into it.

Spelling

2 Decide whether each of these words is spelled correctly or incorrectly. Correct the incorrect ones.

	correct	incorrect	correction
1 recipent	☐	☐	_____
2 addresse	☐	☐	_____
3 to foreward	☐	☐	_____
4 notification of	☐	☐	_____
5 requesting information	☐	☐	_____
6 enquiry	☐	☐	_____
7 complant	☐	☐	_____
8 organize	☐	☐	_____
9 appointment	☐	☐	_____
10 confidensial	☐	☐	_____
11 reciever	☐	☐	_____
12 attachement	☐	☐	_____

VOCABULARY PRACTICE

Pronunciation **3** Look at the letters in bold in these words and phrases. Write the words in the correct column.

thank   get **th**rough   answer **th**e telephone   address **th**e sender   take a message

text   recep**t**ion   confiden**t**ial   no**t**ifica**t**ion   cu**t** off   recipien**t**   at**t**achmen**t**

/t/ as in _table_	/θ/ as in _think_	/ð/ as in _then_	/ʃ/ as in _location_

Collocations **4** Complete each set of collocations with the correct verb.

1 _____ cut off / a message / a call / an e-mail

2 _____ a message / a call

3 _____ a call / an appointment

5 How many verbs can go with each of these nouns?

1 _____ an appointment

2 _____ an e-mail

3 _____ a call

Word families **6** Complete the verb relating to each of the nouns.

noun	verb		noun	verb
1 attachment	a_____	6 notification	n_____
2 recipient	r_____	7 request	r_____
3 reception	r_____	8 complaint	c_____
4 receiver	r_____	9 enquiry	e_____
5 addressee	a_____	10 response	r_____

Consolidation **7** Think of vocabulary relating to telephoning and e-mailing that you might need to understand and/or use.

1 Note it down.

2 Put it into sentences that you are likely to come across.

3 Practise saying and writing them.

 NOW TURN TO YOUR LEARNING JOURNAL AND MAKE NOTES ON THIS SECTION.

Training

★ Before you do these exercises, look at page 73 of the Reference section.

Meaning **I Find words in the word search to complete these sentences.**

1 The handouts or presentation slides form part of the course _____ .

2 When trainers want to see what you have learnt, they may give you a _____ .

3 When a company organizes training, they _____ training courses.

4 'To go on a course' means 'to _____ a course'.

5 Training helps people develop certain _____ , such as becoming better at giving presentations or negotiating.

6 The main aim of training is for the participants to _____ something new.

7 If you have taken a test, you will probably want to know the _____ so you know how well you have done.

8 Bespoke training will establish your _____ before starting the course.

9 A course leading to a qualification may have an _____ instead of a small test.

10 'To train' a person means 'to _____' him/her.

11 If you have to pass an exam, you may have to _____ hard.

12 Most training courses plan in coffee _____ .

13 'Results' means '_____'.

14 A training course may be divided into a number of _____ .

M	A	T	E	R	I	A	L	S	S	I	L
A	V	E	E	U	T	T	H	E	K	L	O
R	D	S	J	N	E	T	S	U	I	S	C
K	L	T	R	I	R	E	S	U	L	T	S
S	E	S	S	I	O	N	S	E	L	E	T
I	A	L	N	E	E	D	S	X	S	A	U
B	R	E	A	K	S	L	F	A	O	C	D
L	N	L	O	W	H	I	M	M	X	H	Y

Spelling **2 Write the past simple and present perfect tenses of these verbs and verb phrases.**

1 attend   7 study

2 take part   8 run

3 participate   9 fund

4 train   10 do well

5 teach   11 fail

6 learn   12 give feedback

For more on past tenses, see page 56.

Pronunciation   **3 Look at the letter _s_ in bold in the words below. Write the words in the correct column(s).**

se**ss**ion   work**sh**op   cour**s**e material**s**   **s**kill**s**   **s**elf-development   te**s**t   mark**s**
pre**ss**ure   **s**tre**ss**   need**s** analy**s**i**s**   a**ss**e**ss**ment   re**s**ult**s**

/s/ as in <u>_study_</u>	/z/ as in <u>_feels_</u>	/ʃ/ as in <u>_show_</u>

VOCABULARY PRACTICE

Collocations   **4 Choose the correct verbs.**

1 _run / make_ a session
2 _make / develop_ skills
3 _do / make_ well
4 _make / take_ an exam

5 _have / do_ a break
6 _make / do_ homework
7 _take / give_ feedback
8 _become / get_ results

5 Choose the correct adverbs.

1 to study _hard / hardly_
2 to do _well / good_
3 to do _badly / bad_
4 to listen _attentively / attendly_

5 to participate _fully / full_
6 to develop skills _quick / quickly_
7 to take part _wantly / willingly_
8 to teach _enthusiastically / enthusiastic_

Word families   **6 Write the verb and noun related to each of these adjectives.**

1 studious
2 participatory
3 trained
4 learned
5 assessed

Consolidation   **7 Think of vocabulary relating to training that you might need to understand and/or use.**

1 Note it down.
2 Put it into sentences that you are likely to come across.
3 Practise saying and writing them.

 NOW TURN TO YOUR LEARNING JOURNAL AND MAKE NOTES ON THIS SECTION.

Present tenses

PRESENT SIMPLE

Form
- Look at how the present simple is formed.

+	subject		+ infinitive (+ –s with he/she/it)	
	My manager		cycles	to work.
–	subject	+ do not (don't) / does not (doesn't)	+ infinitive	
	Staff	don't	start	work early.
?	Do/Does	+ subject	+ infinitive	
	Do	you	enjoy	your job?

- The letter *y* changes to *i*: *I carry* ➜ *he carries*
- Note these short forms: *do not = don't; does not = doesn't*

Use
- The present simple is used to talk about:
  - facts and permanent situations.
    *This branch **doesn't open** until 9 a.m.*
  - routines and schedules.
    *The train **leaves** at 4 p.m.*
- It is often used with time phrases such as *rarely, often, usually, never, on Saturdays, sometimes, every day/week/year.*

PRESENT CONTINUOUS

Form
- Look at how the present continuous is formed.

+	subject	+ to be (am, are, is)	+ infinitive + –ing	
	I	am	working	late tonight.
–	subject	+ to be (am are, is) + not	+ infinitive + –ing	
	We	are not (aren't)	investing	any money.
?	to be (Am, Are, Is)	+ subject	+ infinitive + –ing	
	Are	you	writing	that report?

- Note these short forms:
  I am = I'm; he/she/it is = he's/she's/it's; they are = they're

Use
- The present continuous is used to talk about:
  - activities taking place at or around the time of speaking.
    *We're currently **updating** our HR policies.*
  - temporary or changing situations.
    I'm not working in London long term, just until the end of the year.
  - future arrangements.
    *When **are** you **meeting** Gill for lunch?*
- The present continuous is often used with time phrases such as *now, at the moment, currently, this (year/month/week).*
- One-word time phrases are often placed between *be* and the *–ing* form.
  *I **am currently applying** for a new job.*
- The present continuous is not usually used with these verbs: *hear, think, like, feel, love, believe.*

Past tenses

PAST SIMPLE

Form
- Look at how the past simple is formed.

+	subject		+ infinitive + –ed	
	I		wanted	to change my job.
–	subject	+ didn't	+ infinitive	
	My colleague	didn't	go	to the conference.
?	Did/Didn't	+ subject	+ infinitive	
	Did	you	arrive	on time for the meeting?

- Verbs already ending in *–e* just add *–d*: *decide* ➜ *decided*
- Many verbs are irregular and don't end in *–ed*. (See page 80).
- Note how *did* is used in questions and negative sentences.

Examples
*My company **launched** a new product yesterday.*
*We **didn't finish** work until 6 p.m. last night.*
*Why **didn't** you **come** to the staff party?*

Use
- The past simple is used to talk about:
  - events in the past that are finished.
    *The presentation **took place** two weeks ago.*
  - periods of time in the past that are finished.
    ***Did** you **spend** the whole of last week in Istanbul?*
- The past simple is often used with words such as *last (week/month/year), (two days) ago, yesterday* and *in (2007/January).*

PRESENT PERFECT

Form
- Look at how the present perfect is formed.

+	subject	+ have / has	+ past participle	
	I	have	finished	the project.
–	subject	+ haven't / hasn't	+ past participle	
	My colleagues	haven't	felt	very well lately.
?	Have / Has	+ subject	+ past participle	
	Have	you	seen	the agenda for the meeting?

Examples
I've lost the file on the Staken project.
*We **haven't finished** writing the report.*
***Has** Mikka **left** the organization yet?*

Use
- The present perfect is used to talk about:
  - events that started in the past and are continuing.
    *My boss **has gone** to New York to visit clients.*
  - things that happened in the past that have a strong link with what is happening now (often with *just*).
    *The rise in oil prices **has led** us to increase our own prices.*
- The present perfect is often used with words such as *for (three months / two years), since (Saturday / 1998 / 3 p.m.), already, this (week/month/year), yet, ever/never.*

GRAMMAR REFERENCE

Will and going to

Form: Will
● Look at how sentences using *will* are formed.

+	subject	+ *will*	+ infinitive	
	We	will	pick	*you up at ten.*
–	subject	+ *will not* (*won't*)	+ infinitive	
	I	won't	be	*in tomorrow.*
?	**Will/Won't**	+ subject	+ infinitive	
	Will	you	book	*the meeting room?*

Examples
*By the end of the day, I **will be** exhausted.*
*I **won't be** happy unless I get a pay rise.*
*What **will** Mark **talk** about at the conference?*

Use: Will
● Sentences with *will* are used to:
  – make general predictions.
    *By 11 a.m. tomorrow, I'**ll** probably **be** on the beach.*
  – make spontaneous offers, promises and decisions.
    *I'**ll open** the door for you.*
  – talk about scheduled events.
    *The meeting **will start** at 2.30 p.m.*
● Note that *shall* (*I/we*) can be used to make offers.
  ***Shall** I help you with that?*
  ***Shall** we give Max a lift?*

Form: Going to
● Look at how sentences using *going to* are formed.

+	subject	+ *to be*	+ *going to* + infinitive	
	We	are	going to start	*now.*
–	subject	+ *to be + not*	+ *going to* + infinitive	
	Gill	isn't	going to take	*her exams.*
?	*to be*	+ subject	+ *going to* + infinitive	
	Are	you	going to attend	*the conference next week?*

Examples
*I'**m going to meet** Eleri later.*
*Marcus **isn't going to resign** after all.*
*When **are** the employees **going to leave**?*

Use: Going to
● Sentences with *going to* are used to:
  – talk about a plan or intention.
    *I'**m going to move** to London.*
  – make predictions based on evidence.
    *We'**re going to have** problems – the machine's still broken.*

Modals

Form
● Look at how sentences with modal verbs are formed.

+	subject	+ modal	+ infinitive	
	My colleague	*can*	*speak*	*French fluently.*
–	subject	+ modal + *not*	+ infinitive	
	I	could not (couldn't)	believe	*what I heard.*
?	modal	+ subject	+ infinitive	
	May	I	sit	*here?*

● Modal verbs do not change their form, e.g. they do not take –s in the third person singular.
  I/we/he/she/it/you/they can
● Note these short forms:
  can + not = cannot/can't
  could + not = couldn't
  should + not = shouldn't
  shall + not = shan't
● There is no *to* in the infinitive after modal verbs.
  Staff must keep the equipment clean. (not *to keep*)

Examples
*I **can't understand** this at all.*
*You **shouldn't use** taxis unless absolutely necessary.*
***May** I **ask** you a quick question?*
***Do** I **have to do** that now?*

Use
● Modals are used to:
  – talk about ability (*can*).
    *I **can** speak three foreign languages.*
  – give advice (*should*).
    *You **should** speak to your boss.*
  – make suggestions/offers (*shall*).
    ***Shall** we make a start?*
  – make a polite request (*may / can / could*).
    ***May** I use your office, please?*
  – ask for permission (*may / can / could*).
    ***Could** I start work a bit later, please?*
  – talk about obligation (*have to / must / mustn't*).
    *You **must** fill in your leave form by Friday.*
  – talk about lack of obligation (*don't have to*).
    *We **don't have to** go to work tomorrow.*
  – talk about possibility (*may / might / could*).
    *This project **might** be very complicated.*
● *Shall* is only ever used with the first person (*I* and *we*).
● Of the three verbs *can*, *could* and *may*, *can* is less formal, *could* is neutral and *may* is more formal.
● *Have to* and *must* essentially mean the same, but with *must* the speaker is saying what they think it is necessary to do, while with *have to*, they are talking more about facts.
● *Mustn't* and *don't have to* are totally different.
  You mustn't do something = Don't do it, you are not allowed to do it.
  You don't have to do something = It isn't necessary to do it, but you can if you wish.

Conditionals

Form
- Look at how conditionals are formed.

conditional 1	*if* + present tense,	*will/won't* + infinitive (without *to*)	
	If we leave now,	*we'll arrive*	*on time.*
conditional 2	*if* + past simple,	*would/wouldn't* + infinitive (without *to*)	
	If you reduced the price,	*we would buy*	*the house.*

- You can often use *may/might/could* instead of *will/would*.
  *I **could/might** do more voluntary work if I wasn't so busy.*
  *If I don't get the promotion, I **might/may** leave.*

Use
- Conditionals are used to:
  - talk about future possibilities (conditional 1).
    *If you **speak** to Jane, she'**ll let** you leave early.*
  - give advice and make suggestions (conditional 2).
    *If I **was** you, I **wouldn't take** the job.*
  - talk about imaginary or future situations (conditional 2).
    *If we **had** lots of money, we **would stay** in an expensive resort.*
- It is also correct to say *If I were you ...* instead of *If I was you ...* in conditional 2.
- The *if* part of the clause can come at either the beginning or the end of the sentence. When the *if* clause comes first, it has a comma after it.
  ***If you ring Dampco today,** they'll probably get back to you by tomorrow with a quote.*
  *They'll probably get back to you by tomorrow with a quote **if you ring Dampco today.***

BMG150-TS

'Sometimes I feel the company would collapse if we weren't here.'

www.CartoonStock.com

–*ing* forms and infinitives

Form
- Look at these infinitive forms.

subject + verb		(*not*) *to* + infinitive	
I've asked		*not to work*	*on Terje's project.*
subject + verb	object	(*not*) *to* + infinitive	
We want	*Gill*	*to stay*	*here for a few months.*

- Look at these –*ing* forms.

subject + verb	verb + –*ing*	
I don't enjoy	*doing*	*overtime any more.*

Use
- Infinitives are used:
  - after certain verbs (e.g. *want, hope, need, plan, decide, offer, promise*).
    *Have you **decided to attend** the meeting after all?*
  - after certain verbs + an object (e.g. *ask, tell, warn, expect*).
    *Surely management can't **expect us to work** such long hours.*
  - after adjectives (e.g. *good, wrong*).
    *It's **good to see** you again.*

Examples
*We really **need to increase** sales.*
*My boss hasn't **asked me to go** to the conference.*
*It's **important to have** a good work-life balance.*

- –*ing* forms are used:
  - as nouns (called *gerunds*).
    ***Working** here has been challenging, to say the least.*
    ***Finding** a replacement for Tim will be hard.*
  - after prepositions.
    *Are you interested **in doing** some overtime?*
    *I'm not good **at working** to deadlines.*
  - after certain verbs (e.g. *enjoy, finish, mind, dislike, keep, suggest*).
    *Jamie **suggested going** out for lunch.*
    *I'm going to **keep looking** for a new job.*
- Some verbs can take both infinitives and –*ing* forms with little difference in meaning (e.g. *like, love, hate*).
  I love travelling. = I love to travel.
- However, some verbs (such as *remember, forget, stop*) change their meaning, depending on whether they are followed by the –*ing* form or the infinitive.
  I remembered to send the form. (= I remembered to do it, then I sent it.)
  I remembered sending the form. (= I remembered the act of sending the form.)

GRAMMAR REFERENCE

Comparatives and superlatives

Form: Adjectives and adverbs
● Look at how comparatives and superlatives of adjectives are formed.

	adjective	comparative	superlative
short adjectives (one syllable)	small	*+ –(e)r* smaller	*+ –(e)st* the smallest
longer adjectives ending in –y (two syllables)	easy	*y → i + –(e)r* easier	*y → i + –(e)st* the easiest
longer adjectives not ending in –y (two or more syllables)	important	*more/less + adjective* more important	*the most/least + adjective* the most important

● Look at how comparatives and superlatives of adverbs are formed.

adverb	comparative	superlative
carefully	*more/less + adverb* more carefully	*the most/least + adverb* the most carefully

● Some adjectives have irregular forms.
far–further–the furthest
bad–worse–the worst
good–better–the best
● Some adverbs have irregular forms.
fast–fast
hard–hard
good–well
● The letter *y* at the end of an adjective changes to *i* in front of the superlative and comparative endings.
● The word *than* is used when comparing two things.

Examples
*I find Paris **more interesting than** Rome.*
*Sales of all these perfumes are good, but sales of Enterprise perfume are **the best**.*
*The work is **easier than** I expected.*
*Please could you speak **more clearly**?*

Use
● Comparatives and superlatives are used to:
  – compare two things (comparatives).
    *I am a fast worker, but my colleague is **faster**.*
  – compare three or more things (superlatives).
    *Yesterday was a bad day, and so was the day before, but today is **the worst** day I've had this year!*

Form: Other phrases for making comparisons
● There are other useful phrases for making comparisons.
  the same as
  as ... as
  not as ... as
● Note how the adjectives in these phrases remain unchanged.
  *My desk is **the same** design **as** yours.*
  *Our Frankfurt office is **as successful as** our Hamburg one.*
  *This computer is**n't as expensive as** that one.*

Relative clauses

Form
● Look at the forms used in relative clauses.

	defining clauses	non-defining clauses
who (refers only to people)	*The man **who** you just saw speaks four languages.*	*My line-manager, **who** was late this morning, is off to Belgium on business.*
which (refers only to things)	*The company **which** you used to work for has gone bankrupt.*	*The organization, **which** was founded in 1948, has just been taken over.*
that (refers to people and things)	*The town **that** I come from is called Tiddington.* *The colleague **that** most people admire is Sally.*	
whose (refers to people and things)	*The manager **whose** time-keeping is the worst is Bill.* *The company **whose** sales have fallen most sharply is Concepts.*	*The charity, **whose** income has dropped significantly, is looking for a new funder.* *The CEO, **whose** communication skills are lacking, is going on a negotiation course.*

● *Whom* is only used in formal English. It is used to refer to the object of a clause.
  *The officer to **whom** you should speak is off sick.*
● *Whose* is used to show possession.
● In defining clauses, *who/which* and *that* can generally be used interchangeably.
● *That* is not used in non-defining clauses.

Examples
*We'll be listening to a talk by Sally, **whose** father started the company.*
*Do you want to speak about the changes **that** are soon to take place here?*
*We don't enjoy working with Michael, **who** is our new team leader.*

Use
● **Defining clauses** are used to give essential information about a person or thing.
  *I know the name of the woman **who** applied for the job.*
  *One staff member **whose** work is always exceptional is Jill.*
  *The office **that/which** is at the end of the corridor is the biggest.*
  – *That/which/who* can be left out in defining clauses where the relative pronoun is the object of the clause.
    The man (that/who) I spoke to turned out to be the CEO.
● **Non-defining clauses** are used to give extra, non-essential information about a person or thing.
  *Siobhan, **who** works in finance, has handed in her notice.*
  *Tartu, **which** is in South Estonia, is the location for our next conference.*
  *Maxine, **whose** sales were disappointing in January, won't be team leader next year.*
  – Note the use of commas in non-defining clauses to separate the non-essential information.
    The manager, who is on holiday this week, has been promoted. (Non-defining clause: there is only one manager (who happens to be on holiday this week).)
    The manager who is on holiday this week has been promoted. (Defining clause: there are several managers, but the one we are talking about is the one who is on holiday this week.)

Articles

Form
- *A* is used in front of consonants (*b, c, d,* etc.).
  *He's got **a** big car.*
- *An* is used in front of vowels (*a, e, i, o, u*).
  *This is **an** easy job.*
- *An* is used before words which start with a vowel sound.
  an hour (*h* is silent)
  a hair
  a European (starts with a /j/ sound)

Use
- The indefinite article *a/an* is used to:
  - talk about singular countable nouns.
    *I've just sent **an e-mail** to my boss.*
  - talk about someone's job.
    *He's **an accountant**.*
- *An + other = another*.
  *I've just got **another** job.*
- The definite article *the* is used when:
  - it is clear what you are talking about.
    *He took **the box** down to **the warehouse**.* (a box and warehouse that we know about)
  - you have already mentioned what you are talking about.
    *There's a new job in Finance. **The job** will involve budgeting.*
  - there is only one of something.
    ***The sun** is shining again today.* (There is only one sun.)
  - referring to superlatives.
    *I've got **the best** job in the whole world.*
- No articles are used to:
  - make generalizations.
    ***Unemployment** is rising fast.*
  - talk about general uncountable or plural nouns.
    *There isn't enough **information**.*
- Note these other uses.
  - Continents, cities, countries (except republics, kingdoms, states) do not take an article.
    Africa, Madrid, France, etc.
  - Island groups, regions, republics/kingdoms/states take the definite article.
    the Canaries, the Far East, the United Kingdom, etc.
  - Mountains, oceans/seas, rivers take the definite article.
    the Andes, the Atlantic, the Rhein, etc.
  - Lakes do not take an article.
    Lake Lucerne, Lake Victoria, Lake Eyrie, etc.
  - Compass points and positions take the definite article.
    the north, the south-west, at the top, on the left, etc.
  - Roads and airports do not take an article.
    Victoria Road, Frankfurt Airport, etc.
  - Hotels and cinemas take the definite article.
    the Ibis, the Odeon, etc.
  - Newspapers take the definite article.
    the Guardian, the New York Times, etc.
  - Companies and sectors do not take an article.
    Siemens, electronics, etc.
  - Sports do not take an article.
    football, badminton, etc.
  - Nationalities take the definite article.
    the British, the French, etc.
  - Emergency services take the definite article.
    the police, the fire brigade, etc.
  - Meals do not take an article.
    lunch, dinner, etc.
  - Media usually take the definite article.
    on the radio, but: *on television*

Determiners

Form
- The use of determiners depends on whether the noun they go with are countable or uncountable.
- Countable nouns have singular and plural forms.
  an office, two offices, etc.
- Uncountable nouns have no plural forms.
  finance, information, etc.
- Some nouns have both countable and uncountable forms, with different meanings.
  *Here's **a paper**.* (countable = *a newspaper*)
  *Here's **some paper**.* (uncountable = *writing paper*)

Use
- Look at how determiners are used with countable and uncountable nouns.
  - **some**: in positive sentences with plural countable nouns and uncountable nouns; in requests/offers.
    *We've got **some meetings** next week.*
    *There's **some paper** over here.*
    *Would you like **some cheese**?*
  - **any**: in negative sentences and questions with plural countable nouns and uncountable nouns.
    *Have you got **any information** about the candidates?*
    *I haven't got **any books** on my office shelf.*
  - **much**: in negative sentences and questions with uncountable nouns.
    *They didn't give us **much advice**.*
  - **many**: in negative sentences and questions with plural countable nouns.
    *Staff didn't offer us **many suggestions**.*
  - **a lot of / lots of**: in positive sentences with plural countable nouns and uncountable nouns.
    *There's **a lot of help** available.*
    *I've just eaten **lots of** sweets.*
  - **(a) few**: with plural countable nouns.
    *I've got **a few euros**.*
  - **(a) little**: with uncountable nouns.
    *I've got **little energy** left.*
- Note that:
  - *little/few* are negative ideas.
    *We've got **little** time left.* (= nearly none)
  - *a little / a few* are positive ideas.
    *We've got **a little** time left.* (= not much but some)
- The determiners *any, some* and *no* can be combined with *thing/body/one* to create pronouns.
  anything, something, nothing; anybody, somebody, nobody; anyone, someone, no one

BJH176-TS

'Stan, I've come to trim some of your job benefits.'

Passives

Form
● Look at how the passive is formed.

+	subject	+ *to be*	+ past participle	
	The course	*has been*	*cancelled.*	
–	subject	+ *to be + not*	+ past participle	
	Ginny	*wasn't*	*given*	*promotion.*
?	*(not) to be*	+ subject	+ past participle	
	Was	*Fred*	*met*	*at the station?*

Examples
*Our IT policy **is being reviewed**.*
*Unfortunately, the project **won't be completed** on time.*
*Who **has been given** the job?*

Use
● The passive is used to:
  – emphasize an action, rather than who does it (or if no one knows who does it).
    *Information about the conference **must be sent out** by Wednesday.*
  – describe a system or process.
    *All invoices **are processed** by the finance department.*
  – be formal or impersonal.
    *Members of staff **were requested** to submit their timesheets by the end of the month.*
● *By* can be used to say who carries out an action.
  *Next week's team meeting will be led **by** Marcus Everett.*

'And if we're raided by the Revenue, you make your way here.'

www.CartoonStock.com

Reported speech

Form
● Look at the forms used in reported speech:
  – **tense change**: verbs usually change to the past (e.g. *am/is* → *was*; *are* → *were*; *have/has* → *had*; *can* → *could*; *will* → *would*; *do/does* → *did*; *want* → *wanted*; *come* → *came*)
    *'I **have** an important meeting after lunch.'*
        *She said she **had** an important meeting after lunch.*
    *'We usually **finish** work at 4 p.m.'*
        *He said they usually **finished** work at 4 p.m.*
  – **infinitive with *to*** (e.g. after *tell, agree, ask, decide, expect, refuse*)
    'I'm sorry, but you can't attend the training course.'
    *My boss **refused to let** me attend the training course.*
  – **–*ing* form** (e.g. after *admit, suggest, deny*)
    'Shall we have a catch-up this afternoon?'
    *My colleague **suggested having** a catch-up that afternoon.*
  – **object + infinitive with *to*** (e.g. after *advise, ask, invite, tell, warn*)
    'Don't forget to phone Jessy about the product launch.'
    *Jeremy **reminded me to phone** Jessy about the product launch.*

Examples
*She said she **didn't want** to come with us.*
*He **told me to wait** for five minutes.*
*They **invited us to attend** the conference.*

● These common time changes are used in reported speech:
  now → *then*; *yesterday* → *the day before*; *ago* → *before*; *this (week)* → *that (week)*; *tomorrow* → *the next/following day*
● However, if the 'reporting' takes place in the same period, the time reference stays the same.
  *'We launched the new product **yesterday**.'*
  *She told me they launched the new product **yesterday**.*
  (reported on the same day as the statement was made)
● If you are reporting something and you think that it is still true, you don't need to change the tense to the past.
  *'I **like** living in Madrid.'*
  *She said she **likes** living in Madrid.*
● Watch out for pronouns – they also need to change (usually from first person to third person).
  *'**I**'m going to send her **my** report tomorrow.'*
  ***He** said **he** was going to send her **his** report the next day.*
● It is not always necessary to include *that*.
  He said (that) he felt tired.

Use
● Reported speech is used to tell someone what you/someone else said.

Examples
*Siraj told Atul she **wouldn't cover** his shift for him.*
*The team leader said I **didn't have to** work afternoons.*
*I **reminded Jo to take** some leave.*

Companies and offices

Meaning

Here are some definitions and examples of vocabulary relating to companies and offices.

competitive – when a company offers good products or services at a good rate

to close offices – to cease trading from premises when a business no longer needs as many offices, perhaps due to less demand or because of rising costs

to expand into new markets – to start operating in new regions or countries

a good reputation – when a company is respected and valued by people

a hot desk – a desk usually used by contractors, one which does not have a specific employee associated with it

to merge – to combine to become one (e.g. two companies)

a multinational company – a company that operates in more than one country

on the third floor – when an office is on level 3 or on the third storey of a building

open-plan – when an office has no interior walls, so that all members of staff are working in the same room rather than in individual offices

the production industry – companies that produce goods (e.g. cars, steel, plastics)

profitable – when a business makes a profit and is not loss-making

to be recognized internationally – to be known about and well thought-of around the world

a security pass – a card allowing entry to premises or building, possibly with a photo of the holder

the service industry – companies that offer a service (e.g. training, leisure, marketing)

a solid client base – a number of reliable and regular clients/customers

to take over – to buy another company

to trade (in) – to do business (in a particular field)

a tower block – a building with very many floors

an upcoming company – a new company making an impression on the market

a well-established company – a company that has been in business long enough to have a solid client base and good reputation

the working environment – the place and atmosphere within which people work

> Notice the prepositions used: *expand **into**, **on** the third floor, trade **in** stocks and shares.*

> *To take over* can also be used in the sense of taking over responsibility: *Mike is going **to take over** the role of Chief Buyer when Shirley retires.*

Examples

We've expanded into exciting new markets in the Far East and we are starting to be recognized internationally.

RightFix, a relatively new and upcoming company offering domestic repair services, already has quite a solid client base and a good reputation.

Our small, family-run business just can't compete with large, profitable multinationals.

Spelling

When spelling vocabulary relating to companies and offices, remember:

● that a final *e* is sometimes dropped in verb forms. *merge – merging, take over – taking over*

● irregular verbs: *take over – took over – taken over; shrink – shrank – shrunk*

● that British and American spelling sometimes differs. *to be **recognised** internationally* (UK) – *to be **recognized** internationally* (US)

Pronunciation

When speaking, think about sounds that run together, including between separate words. Sounds often run together when a consonant sound precedes a vowel sound.

clos**e o**ffices	/zɒ/	ta**ke o**ver	/kəʊ/
expan**d i**nto new markets	/dɪ/	workin**g e**nvironment	/ŋɪ/
recognize**d e**verywhere	/de/		

Compare the above phrases with the following ones where the sounds between the two words do not run together. This is usually because the first word ends with a consonant sound and the next word starts with a consonant sound.

goo**d r**eputation	well-know**n c**ompany
multinationa**l c**ompany	thir**d f**loor

Collocations

Here are different verbs and nouns that can be used with some key vocabulary (in **bold**) relating to companies and offices.

an upcoming / well-known / internationally recognized / multinational **company**

a(n) open-plan / old-fashioned / modern / well-designed **office**

a pleasant / stressful / friendly / noisy **working environment**

a profitable / reputable / successful / struggling **business**

a production / service / tertiary / secondary / primary / struggling / booming **industry**

Examples

Rafael works in a large, open-plan office, which he finds quite noisy.

The government is trying to support struggling businesses.

I prefer working for a multinational company because I have the chance to work in different countries.

Word families

The table shows how some nouns, verbs and adjectives in the area of companies relate to one another.

noun	verb	adjective
competition	to compete	competitive
decline	to decline	declining
expansion	to expand	expanding, expandable
growth	to grow	growing
merger	to merge	merging, merged
profit	to make a profit	profitable
reputation	to have a reputation	reputable
shrinkage	to shrink	shrinking
trade	to trade	trading

Examples

*We are making the most of the **shrinking** market.* (adjective)

*Despite being a multinational company, business **has shrunk** over the last two years.* (verb)

*We are merging with a **reputable** company.* (adjective)

*A bad write-up can harm a company's **reputation**.* (noun)

Finance

Meaning
Here are some definitions and examples of vocabulary relating to finance.

to be up by 30% – to have increased by 30%

a cost – an amount of money a company or person has to pay to buy something

to decrease – to fall; to drop; to go down

to drop – to decrease; to go down

the economic climate – the situation in which the economy finds itself

to even out – to become more stable, having previously fallen or increased (e.g. costs or sales)

an exact figure – a figure which is known precisely, so often used when talking about figures in the past

to fall – to decrease; to drop

a financial forecast – a prediction, looking to the future as to what the financial situation will be

to increase – to go up; to rise

interest rates – the percentage that determines the amount of interest that people and companies have to pay (e.g. when they borrow money)

an investment – something in which money is invested for the future

a loan – an amount of money that is borrowed, usually from a bank

a long-term outlook – when you look ahead to the distant future (e.g. when predicting how well a company will do in ten years' time, rather than just in the next six months)

market instability – when a market is not very stable

market stability – when a market is stable

to nose-dive – to go down or drop rapidly

overheads – costs that a company has to pay all the time, such as salaries, electricity and rent

to predict – to forecast; to say what you think will happen in the future

profitable – when a product or service makes a profit

to rise – to increase; to go up

to rocket – to increase rapidly

a rough figure – a figure which is not known precisely, so often an estimate for talking about figures in the future

share prices – the costs to buy or sell shares

total sales figures – the complete number of items sold

unprofitable – not profitable

> Notice the difference between *economic* and *economical*. *Economic* relates to the economy and *economical* means 'not needing much of something'.

Examples
Higher interest rates mean that companies are finding it harder to pay off loans.

Overheads are continuing to rise, and total sales figures have dropped by 15%, so it is unprofitable to keep business as it is.

Experts predict that share prices will gradually even out, and so the long-term outlook is positive for investment.

Sales have nose-dived over the last few months, resulting in market instability.

Spelling
When spelling vocabulary in the field of finance, remember:
- irregular verb forms: *rise* → *rose*, *fall* → *fell*
- adjectives are formed from nouns in different ways: *stability* → *stable*, *economy* → *economic*, *profit* → *profitable*
- negative forms of adjectives and/or nouns often add *un–* or *in–* as prefixes: *profitable* → *unprofitable*, *stability* → *instability*

Pronunciation
When speaking, think about how you pronounce certain letters and sounds. The letter *o* has different sounds in different words.

/ɒ/: to r**o**cket, to dr**o**p, pr**o**fit, c**o**st, l**o**ng-term

/əʊ/: to n**o**se-dive, **o**verheads, t**o**tal sales figures, l**oa**ns

/ɔː/: f**o**recast, f**o**resee, b**oa**rd meeting, sh**o**rtage, s**ou**rce

Collocations
Here are different verbs, nouns and adjectives that can be used with some key vocabulary (in **bold**) relating to finance.

overhead / investment / rising / falling / marketing / sales / production / distribution / recruitment **costs**

to decrease / increase / spread out **costs**

exact / long-term / rough / sales / short-term / total **figures**

to double-check / finalize / look into / predict **figures**

to forecast / improve / promote **sales**

Examples
Production costs have been rising steadily over the last five years.

We plan to spread out costs for promoting sales throughout the year rather than have a large investment in springtime, even though this is what our competitors do.

At this stage, I can only give you rough figures of what the repair work will cost. When I have completed my assessment, I can provide more exact figures.

Word families
The table shows how some nouns and verbs in the area of finance have the same form.

noun	verb
a decrease	to decrease
a drop	to drop
a fall	to fall
a nose dive	to nose-dive
a rise	to rise
an increase	to increase

Examples
We have experienced a drop in sales and we expect they will continue to drop for the foreseeable future unless we do something about it.

Although overhead costs have been increasing since the beginning of the year, the Head of Finance doesn't expect the increase to continue beyond the end of summer.

Human resources

Meaning
Here are some definitions and examples of vocabulary relating to human resources.

annual leave – the time an employee can take for holidays each year and still be paid

to apply for a job – to send a CV and personal information to a potential employer to try and get work with them

an appraisal – an (often) annual meeting between boss and member of staff to discuss achievements and problems and to plan ahead

an appraisee – a person having an appraisal

an appraiser – a person doing an appraisal

to be made redundant – to lose your job because of economic or restructuring reasons

a candidate – a person being interviewed and considered for a vacant post

to employ – to give someone a job and pay them a salary

an employee – a person who is employed

an employer – a person, company or organization who employs someone

to give notice – to inform an employer that you are leaving your job

a job application – when a potential candidate informs an employer that he/she is interested in a vacant post and supplies information about skills and experience

to join a company – to start working for a company

to leave a company – to stop working for a company

a pension scheme – when an employer or employee pays money into a specific account for use when the employee retires

to recruit – to take on new members of staff, usually after a selection process (e.g. after interviews)

recruitment – the taking-on of new members of staff

to retire – to stop working and draw on a pension, usually when you get older

salary – the money an employee earns in a year

sick leave – when an employee is not able to work due to ill health

staff development – training offered to members of staff to develop their skills

a union – an organization that supports and represents the rights of workers

a vacancy / a vacant position – a job that is not filled

> Notice the difference in meaning between *employee* and *employer*, and between *appraisee* and *appraiser*.

> When employees stop working later in life, they *retire*. The money they receive is their *pension*.

Examples
John was looking for a better-paid job, so he applied for a vacant position in Head Office.

Many employees were made redundant as a result of production costs being too high in Europe.

The union is encouraging management to invest more in staff development so members of staff can do their jobs more easily.

During his appraisal, John informed his appraiser that he was planning to take four weeks' annual leave in September so he could visit his relatives in Australia.

Having looked at the job applications, there are six suitable candidates, and we're hoping to recruit one of them by the end of the month.

Spelling
When spelling vocabulary in the field of human resources, remember:
- that *y* sometimes changes to *i* in these situations:
  - verb → noun: *apply* → *application*
  - verb forms: *apply* → *applies/applied* (BUT *applying*)
  - plurals: *salary* → *salaries*, *vacancy* → *vacancies*
- irregular verbs: *leave (a company)* → *left (a company)*
- uncountable nouns (no plural form): *(staff) development*, *(to give) notice*, *(annual/sick) leave*

Pronunciation
When speaking, think about word stress.
- Notice how the stress within these words stays the same for both the verb and the noun form:
  *to re**cruit** – re**cruit**ment*
  *to ap**praise** – ap**prais**al*
  *to em**ploy** – em**ploy**er/em**ploy**ment*
- However, the stress within these words changes between the verb and noun:
  *to ap**ply** – an appli**ca**tion*
  *to em**ploy** – an employ**ee***

Collocations
Here are different verbs and nouns that can be used with some key vocabulary (in **bold**) relating to human resources.

to be signed off on / go off on / take **sick leave**
to belong to / be a member of / join **a union**
to apply for / advertise / fill **a vacant post**
recruitment process / figures

Examples
Stefan was signed off on sick leave for three weeks.
Are you a member of a union?
Recruitment figures for the north of the region have gone up in the last six months.

Word families
The table shows how some nouns, verbs and adjectives in the area of human resources relate to one another.

noun	verb	adjective
application	to apply for	applicable
appraisal	to appraise	
(staff) development	to develop	
employment	to employ	employable
employee		
employer		
recruitment	to recruit	recruitable
redundancy	to be made redundant*	redundant
	to make someone redundant*	

*Strictly speaking, these are verb phrases, not verbs in their own right.

Examples
*The result of the interviews was that no one was perfect, but two candidates were **recruitable**.* (adjective)
*Can you send in your **application** with a covering letter stating why you should be considered for the job?* (noun)
*My line manager is very busy at the moment, as she is having to **appraise** six people in the next two weeks.* (verb)

Logistics

Meaning

Here are some definitions and examples of vocabulary relating to logistics.

a batch – a group of products handled together, often having come off the production line at the same time

a bulk order – a large order, often containing several different items

by rail – when goods are transported by train

by sea – when goods are transported by ship

confirmation of delivery – when the customer acknowledges with the supplier receipt of delivery (i.e. that he/she has received the goods)

a consignment – a shipment of goods

a container – a box on the back of a lorry that can be loaded from one means of transport to another

customs – when imported goods are examined at a border in case any duty needs to be paid

to deliver – to supply the finished products to the customer

a delivery – a consignment or products being delivered

a discount – when a lower price is offered (e.g. when a large order is placed)

to dispatch/despatch – to send a delivery out from the warehouse

freight – cargo; goods transported, often by a slower – and therefore less expensive – means of transport

goods – products; items

to have in stock – to have finished goods in the warehouse ready for delivery

insurance – financial protection in case a consignment is lost, delayed or damaged

an invoice – a document showing the final amount owing

a lorry – a large road vehicle that can transport containers by road

to mail out – to send (often small) goods out by post

to order – to request products or services to be delivered

a pallet – a wooden tray on which goods for delivery can be stacked and then moved by fork-lift truck

to pay in full – to pay the entire amount owing

to pay in instalments – to pay the amount owing in stages, perhaps a small amount each month

to purchase – to buy (e.g. supplies or end products)

a shipment – when goods are shipped or transported together

to supply – to provide materials or services so that production can take place

transport costs – the money needed to send goods by road, rail, sea or air

a unit price – how much a single item costs

a warehouse – where finished goods are stored before delivery

> Do not confuse *customs* with *customers*.

Examples

If we have the items in stock, we can dispatch your order today.

It makes sense to take out insurance when shipping goods overseas. You never know if there will be delays at customs or if the consignment will get damaged as it is moved from lorry to ship.

JBC Electronics plc usually give good discounts for bulk orders.

I'd like to confirm receipt of delivery, order number XP-0912, and to let you know we'll pay the invoice in full by the end of the month.

Freight transport costs have increased recently, so we might need to look into other options.

Spelling

When spelling vocabulary in the field of logistics, remember:

- that *y* sometimes changes to *i*:
  - verb → noun: *supply → supplier*
  - verb forms: *supply → supplies/supplied* (BUT *supplying*)
  - plural: *supply → supplies, delivery → deliveries*
  - adjective → adverb: *speedy → speedily*
- irregular verbs: *pay → paid, have in stock → had in stock*
- uncountable nouns have no plural: *insurance*
- British and American spelling sometimes differs:

UK	US
despatch	*dispatch*
instalment	*installment*

Pronunciation

When speaking, take care to make the distinction between the sounds /tʃ/ and /ʃ/.

- The sound /tʃ/ is often denoted by the letters *ch: ba**tch**, pur**ch**ase*
- The sound /ʃ/ is often denoted by the letters *sh, sur + vowel, cial or tion*: **sh**ip, in**sur**e, finan**cial**, confirma**tion**.

Collocations

Here are different verbs and nouns that can be used with some key vocabulary (in **bold**) relating to logistics.

to place / put in **an order**

to have in stock / to store **in the warehouse**

to pay in full / instalments / cash

to pay by bank transfer / cheque

to order / mail out / deliver **goods**

to transport freight / goods / a consignment / by road / by rail / by sea

Examples

Nicky mailed out the replacement goods as soon as she received the request.

Freight is usually transported as cheaply as possible to keep profit margins up.

We normally request that new customers pay in full.

Word families

The table shows how some adjectives and adverbs can be used in relation to logistics, and how the adjectives and adverbs relate to one another.

adjective	adverb
considerate	considerately
direct	directly
fast	fast
immediate	immediately
slow	slowly
speedy	speedily
swift	swiftly

Note that *fast* has the same form, whether it is an adjective or an adverb.

Examples

*We need **immediate** action to solve this logistics problem.* (adjective)

*The warehouse will dispatch the goods **immediately**.* (adverb)

*That was a **speedy** response to my request to place an order with you – thank you!* (adjective)

*The administrator dealt with the invoices **speedily** and efficiently.* (adverb)

Meetings and conferences

Meaning

Here are some definitions and examples of vocabulary relating to meetings and conferences.

an appointment – an arranged meeting with someone, e.g. bank manager, customer

to arrange a meeting – to organize a meeting, such as inviting participants and booking the venue

to attend a meeting – to take part in a meeting

an attendee – a person who attends a meeting

to book a room – to reserve a room (e.g. to use for a meeting)

to cancel a venue – to withdraw a booking when the room or location of a meeting or conference is no longer needed

to collect in forms – to take back forms, such as feedback forms or questionnaires, from participants of a conference

to disagree – to not have the same opinion as someone else

a graph – a diagram which may have lines or bars representing figures, such as sales over time

to hold a meeting – to have a meeting

to make a suggestion – to make a proposal; to put an idea forward

to miss a meeting – to fail to attend a meeting, even though you intended to, perhaps because you are held up in traffic or an earlier meeting runs on longer than you expected

the minutes – the report or summary from a meeting, often showing action points and when they are to be done and by whom

to negotiate – to try and reach agreement with a partner who may have different objectives to your own, often involving the need to compromise

to organize a conference – to arrange a conference

to pass round handouts – to give papers (possibly photocopies) to participants of a meeting or conference

a participant – a person who attends or takes part in a meeting or conference

to participate in – to take part in; to attend; to be present at

to postpone – to push the date of a meeting or conference back to a later date

a projector – a piece of equipment that shows the computer screen on the wall or bigger screen so that a large number of people can see it

to reach an agreement – to finally have the same opinion; to agree in the end after a discussion or negotiation

a videoconference – a conference with audio and visual input held at a distance via the Internet

a visual – something like a graph, chart, diagram or photograph, used perhaps to support a point being made in a presentation

to voice an opinion – to say what you think

> Notice the prepositions in the following: *participate in a meeting, take part in a meeting, be present at a meeting, attend a meeting* (no preposition).

Examples

OK, I've arranged the team meeting for Thursday. I've booked the meeting room on the first floor and have asked for the projector to be set up for us to use.

Klaus-Dieter and his business partner finally reached agreement over distribution costs after negotiating by e-mail and telephone.

I'm sorry, I was held up and missed the meeting today. Can you send me the minutes so I can see what was agreed?

Have we prepared enough handouts to pass round to the participants?

Spelling

When spelling vocabulary in the field of meetings and conferences, remember:
- double consonants: a**pp**ointment, questio**nn**aire
- sounds have different spellings: /ʃ/ **sh**ow, nego**tia**te /f/ con**f**erence, **ph**otocopy
- some words do not have a singular form: minute**s**

Pronunciation

- The sound /ə/ (schwa) is very common in spoken English. It is a short, unstressed sound.
- Notice that the letters and combination of letters vary, but often the following are pronounced /ə/:
  - *–er* or *–or* at the end of a word when the syllable is not stressed: speak**er**, project**or**
  - *–er* in the middle of a word that is not stressed: int**er**view
  - the letter *a* at the beginning of a word or in the middle of a word when the *a* is not the stressed syllable: **a**ppointment, dis**a**gree
  - the indefinite article *a* in a sentence where it is not stressed for importance of meaning: lead **a** discussion
  - the *e* in *–el* at the end of a word when the syllable is not stressed: canc**e**l

Collocations

Here are different verbs and nouns that can be used with some key vocabulary (in **bold**) relating to meetings and conferences.

to reach / postpone **an agreement**
to reach / postpone **a conclusion**
to fill in a form / a questionnaire
to write up a report / the minutes
to book a room / a venue
to cancel a room / a venue / a meeting
to take the minutes / notes
to attend / hold / postpone / arrange **a meeting**
to make / postpone / cancel **an appointment**

Examples

Tita wrote up the minutes after attending the project progress meeting.

If you attend the conference, could you please fill in the questionnaire and hand it back HR, so they can decide whether to send other people in the future?

Despite holding a meeting, management postponed any agreement.

Word families

Nouns can be made from verbs by adding certain endings. Here are some typical endings of nouns in the area of meetings and conferences.
- *–ment* (disagree → disagreement)
- *–(t)ion* – if the verb ends in *s*, then no *t* is added (present → presentation, discuss → discussion)
- *–er* or *–or* (present → presenter, direct → director)
- *–ant* (participate → participant)
- *–ance* (attend → attendance)
- *–ing* (book → booking)

Examples

*Jens usually **participates** in the staff development conference.* (verb)

*There were fewer **participants** at this year's conference.* (noun)

*We're here to **discuss** potential redundancies and what we can do to avoid them.* (verb)

*The **discussion** was lively, but no agreement could be reached.* (noun)

People and places

Meaning
Here are some definitions and examples of vocabulary relating to people and places.

an assistant – someone who supports someone above them, such as a Technical Assistant who assists the Technical Director

to be based in – to be located somewhere; to have your company in a particular place

a call centre – a place where people work on telephones answering calls from customers

a central location – in the town or city centre

a colleague – someone you work with; a co-worker

an employee – someone who works for someone else (who is their employer)

an employer – a person, company or organization who employs someone

a factory – a building or series of buildings which house production of some kind

Head of Sales – the person in charge of sales

an industrial estate – an area where several factories, offices or distribution centres are located all together

a manager – a person who is responsible for a department, team or project

an office – a place where business is carried out, usually consisting of a room or rooms with desks where members of staff work

on the outskirts – on the edge of a town or city

premises – where a business is located (the offices, workshop or factory)

to report to – to have a manager or someone above you in the hierarchy to whom you are responsible

rural – in the countryside

the shop floor – the part of a factory where the production takes place

a subordinate – a worker who reports to someone above them in the hieracrchy

a team leader – a person who is in charge of a team; a manager of a team

a warehouse – a place where finished goods are stored before being distributed

> Notice the difference between *employee* and *employer*.

> Notice the meaning of *shop floor* here. *Shop floor* can also be used to refer to the area in a shop where items are sold.

Examples
We moved to new premises on an industrial estate on the outskirts of Milton Keynes.

The Head of Production usually goes onto the shop floor every day so he can speak to the workers.

The warehouse really needs to have a central location, but rents are too expensive.

All secretaries report to the Head of Administration.

Spelling
When spelling vocabulary relating to people and places, remember that:
- *y* sometimes changes to *i*:
  - verb → noun: *apply* → *application*
  - verb forms: *study* → *studies/studied* (BUT *studying*)
  - plurals: *secretary* → *secretaries, economy* → *economies*

- countable nouns add *–s* or *–es* in the plural: *manager* → *managers, employee* → *employees, boss* → *bosses*
- some nouns are only used in the plural form: *premises, outskirts*
- uncountable nouns have no plural form: *law, science*
- job titles often have initial capital letters: *Head of Finance, Technical Advisor*

Pronunciation
When speaking, think about the pronunciation of the letter *a*. It has different sounds and is often pronounced:
- /eɪ/ as in *pay* when it:
  - is followed by the letter *y*: *pay, say, delay*
  - occurs between two consonants followed by the letter *e*: *sales, locate, page*
- /eə/ as in *fair* when it is:
  - followed by *ir*: *fair, air, chair*
  - preceded by a consonant and followed by the letters *re*: *share, warehouse*
- /æ/ as in *factory* when it is followed by a consonant (and no *e* after it): *an, man, manager*
- /ɑ:/ as in *farther* when it is followed by an *r*, or *r* and another consonant: *car, partner*
- /ə/ as in *attend* when the sound is not stressed: *cent**a**l, **a**ssist**a**nt*

Collocations
Here are different nouns and adjectives that can be used with some key vocabulary (in **bold**) relating to people and places.

call / development / distribution / financial / training **centre**
central / easily accessible / industrial / pretty / rural **location**
distribution / finance / sales / team **manager**
Head of Development / Finance / Sales / Training

Examples
As Head of Sales, Rupert has 14 salespeople working for him.

When looking for our new office, our priority was an easily accessible location so that our customers could call in whenever they wanted.

Have you seen the designs for the new training centre? It should be so much better than the old one.

Word families
- Professions can be formed from verbs or nouns by adding:
  - *–er* to the stem of the verb:
    buy → *buyer, manage* → *manager*
  - *–or* to the stem of the verb:
    coordinate → *coordinator, advise* → *advisor*
  - *–ant* to the stem of the verb: *assist* → *assistant*
  - *–ist* to the base form of the noun:
    economy → *economist, science* → *scientist*
- Note that *lawyer* is the profession relating to *law*, and *engineer* relates to *engineering*.

> The indefinite article is usually used with professions and job titles: *She is a lawyer. He is a teacher.*

Examples
*Sarah's responsibility is to **buy** all materials needed for redevelopment projects.* (verb) *She is a **buyer**.* (profession)

*Valérie **assists** Pierre in organizing training courses at RP Electrics.* (verb) *She is the Training **Assistant**.* (profession)

*Anne studied **science** at Sheffield University.* (verb) *She is a **scientist**.* (profession)

Planning

Meaning

Here are some definitions and examples of vocabulary relating to planning.

achievable – something that is realistic and possible, such as a goal

to analyze – to look into something in detail, such as why sales have not risen as much as hoped

to base a decision on – to make a decision depending on information available at the time

to be cautious – to be careful; to not want to take big risks

a concern – a worry, something you're not very confident or happy about

to conduct an assessment – to analyze; to carry out research, perhaps to feed into the decision-making process

the current situation – what things are like now, at the present time

to diversify – to move into new or different areas of work

to downsize – to become smaller

to draw up a plan – to put a plan together

to enable – to make something possible; to make something happen

to evaluate – to assess a situation; to look at pros and cons

to expand – to get bigger; to move into more markets

a failure – something that didn't go well, wasn't a success

to focus on – to concentrate on; to have as the main thing to work on

a forecast – a prediction; how you think things might turn out in the future

a goal – an objective; what is to be aimed at (and hopefully achieved) in the future

to look into – to get more information about; to consider

to make the most of – to get as many benefits out of a situation as possible

an outlook – a probable or expected outcome

to pan out – to work out; to turn out

the planning process – the stages to go through when planning

to predict – to say how things might turn out in the future

a priority – an action that needs to be done before another

a proposal – a suggestion; an idea; a possible way forward

to raise a concern – to express a worry

a risk – something you cannot control, but which could have a negative effect

to set targets – to agree what is achievable and what should be done

to share a vision – to have the same idea about what should be done and achieved in the future

a strategy – an agreed way forward; a plan for success

a success – something that goes well, as planned

unforeseen – something that was not expected

unrealistic – something that is not particularly achievable

Examples

When setting targets, you should analyze the market and take risks into consideration. Then, to complete the planning process, decide which actions are priorities.

Due to concerns about the economic climate and customer demands, TT Motors plan to downsize and focus on producing environmentally friendly small cars.

Spelling

When spelling vocabulary relating to planning, remember:
- that a final *e* is sometimes dropped:
  - verb forms: *analyze* → *analyzing*, *enable* → *enabling*

- that a *y* sometimes becomes an *i*:
  - verb forms: *diversify* → *diversifies* → *diversified*
  - plural nouns: *strategy* → *strategies*
- irregular verbs: *draw up (a plan)* → *drew up* → *drawn up*; *set (targets)* → *set* → *set* (See page 80.)
- that British and American spelling sometimes differs: *analyse* → *analyze*

Pronunciation

When speaking, think about the pronunciation of the letter *r*.
- It is usually pronounced /r/ at the beginning of a word or when it follows a consonant: **r**isk, **r**aise, cur**r**ent, p**r**edict
- It is not usually pronounced when it follows a vowel, including at the end of the word: conce**r**n /kən'sɜːn/, failu**r**e /'feɪljə/, fo**r**ecast /'fɔːkɑːst/, slowe**r** /'sləʊ(w)ə/.
- Note that there are some regional accents where the *r* may be pronounced in the middle of a word or at the end, e.g. dive**r**sify, neve**r**.
- An *r* at the end of a word is pronounced if the following word starts with a vowel sound: fewe**r** offices /'fjuːər'ɒfɪsɪz/.

Collocations

Here are different verbs and nouns that can be used with some key vocabulary (in **bold**) relating to planning.

to predict / plan for / forecast / set targets for **the future**
to assess / manage / accept / avoid **risks**
to set goals / targets / priorities
to draw up plans / strategies
achievable / realistic / unrealistic / high-risk / low-risk **goals**

Examples

Our Head of Planning is currently setting targets for our company. He is focusing on the next three years.
There are too many unrealistic goals.
We need to be careful when setting our priorities. The decision could make or break us.

Word families

The table shows how some adjectives and adverbs, which can be used to talk about planning, relate to one another. Some describe manner, some describe time.

adjective	adverb
achievable	
ambitious	ambitiously
cautious	cautiously
current	currently
high-risk	
low-risk	
immediate	immediately
optimistic	optimistically
pessimistic	pessimistically
present	presently
realistic	realistically
unforeseen	

Examples

*Our Managing Director set very **cautious** targets for the next six to nine months.* (adjective)
*Given the current economic climate, which isn't good, Andrew **cautiously** agreed to open two more stores in the southern region.* (adverb)

Production and processes

Meaning

Here are some definitions and examples of vocabulary relating to production and processes.

to deliver – to supply finished products to the customer

a delivery – a consignment or products being delivered

a factory – where production takes place

health and safety procedures – rules to ensure workers are not injured during production (e.g. the wearing of a hard hat and safety goggles)

high quality – good quality; describing products that will be durable and well designed

to implement a procedure – to put a process in place

to install – to put new machinery in place

just-in-time (JIT) production – producing goods just in time for delivery, to avoid warehouse costs

machinery – machines and equipment

to maintain – to keep machinery in good working order

maintenance – the upkeep of machinery through cleaning and repairing

to meet a deadline – to keep to a scheduled date

a procedure – a way of working; a process

a process – a system; a way of working

to produce – to manufacture; to make

a product – the end result or outcome of producing something; goods

to purchase – to buy (e.g. supplies or end products)

quality assurance (QA) – a procedure that aims to ensure the high quality of a product by testing and considering throughout production what makes the product good

to schedule production – to put a timeframe to what needs to be produced; to set milestone dates/deadlines, etc.

to have in stock – to have finished goods in the warehouse ready for delivery

a supplier – a person or company who provides materials or services so that production can take place

to test an initial batch – to check the first products off the production line; to put them though their paces

a trial run – when a sample batch of a new product is released onto the market

a unit – the smallest denominator of what is produced, and item

to update a system – to bring a system up to date; to modernize it

a warehouse – where finished goods are stored before delivery

to work shifts – to work set patterns round the clock in a factory to enable production to continue

> The word *produce* can also be used as a noun, often to refer to food stuffs. But note that the stress falls on the first syllable when it's a noun.

Examples

Antonio works shifts at R.P. Electronics. He prefers the day shift, as he can spend time with his children in the evening, but he has to work the night shift every third week.

Maintenance costs have risen over the last few years, and it's becoming increasingly difficult to get replacement parts for the machines.

Even visitors have to follow the health and safety procedures, and safety goggles have to be worn at all times.

We've moved to just-in-time production, which means the warehouse will close, and 35 staff will lose their jobs.

The trial run proved that we had succeeded in producing high-quality goods.

Spelling

When spelling vocabulary in the field of production and processes, remember:

● that *y* sometimes changes to *i*:
 – verb → noun: *supply → supplier*
 – verb forms: *supply → supplies/supplied* (BUT *supplying*)
 – plural: *supply → supplies*, *delivery → deliveries*
● irregular verbs: *meet a deadline → met a deadline, have in stock → had in stock*
● uncountable nouns have no plural: *machinery, quality, maintenance*

Pronunciation

When speaking, think about word stress.

● Notice how the stress in these words stays the same for both the verb and the noun form:
 – to **pro**cess → **pro**cess
 – to **sche**dule → **sche**dule
 – to **pur**chase → **pur**chase
● However, the stress in these words changes between the verb and noun:
 – to in**stall** → an instal**la**tion
 – to main**tain** → **main**tenance
 – to pro**duce** → a **pro**duct, fresh **pro**duce (BUT pro**duc**tion)

Collocations

Here are different verbs and nouns that can be used with some key vocabulary (in **bold**) relating to production and processes.

to place / put in **an order**
to follow / implement **procedures**
to have in stock / store **in the warehouse**
an increase / a decrease in **production costs**
to assure / test **quality**
to do / get feedback on **a trial run**
to keep to / set up **a schedule**

Examples

HR implemented new procedures for logging time worked on shifts.
How do you test quality on new products?
Exactly how many have we got in stock in the warehouse?

Word families

The table shows how some nouns and verbs in the area of production and processes relate to one another.

noun	verb
delivery	to deliver
maintenance	to maintain
process, procedure	to process
product, production, (produce)	to produce
purchase, purchasing	to purchase
schedule	to schedule
supply	to supply
update	to update

Examples

*We need to **maintain** our machinery on a regular basis.* (verb)
*Production has slowed due to **maintenance** of the conveyor belts.* (noun)
*I know you work for HG Plastics, but what exactly do you **produce**?* (verb)
*Our **products** have won awards for innovation.* (noun)

Projects and teams

Meaning
Here are some definitions and examples of vocabulary relating to projects and teams.

to brief someone – to explain to someone (often a contractor or a member of a team) what he/she needs to do

a consignment – a number of items delivered at the same time

a contractor – a person who is not an employee but who may work on a project on a temporary basis, perhaps because of his/her specific skills

a deadline – a date by which work on a project needs to be done

a delay – when production is slower than scheduled

to deliver – to transport goods to the customer

to estimate costs – to say what you think the costs of a project will be

modifications – changes made to a design or product

progress – work done on a project that moves it forward

a project manager – a person in charge of a project, who ensures that work is carried out in time, to budget and of the quality required

to reorganize – to organize something again (e.g. to change the date of a scheduled meeting)

a schedule – a time plan within which work on a project needs to be done

to see a project through – to ensure a project is finished; to take a project to the end

skills – knowledge and abilities in a particular area (e.g. in computing or in administration)

specifications – requirements for the project, specifying what needs to be done

to support – to work with and help other people (e.g. other team members)

to sign a contract – to put your name to a contract signalling that you agree with it

a team member – a person who is part of a team

to underestimate costs – to say that costs will be lower than they really are

> *Brief* can also be used as an adjective to mean 'short': *a brief summary*. *Project* can also be used as a verb: *to project figures*.

Examples
Jenny is going to brief the contractor when he comes in tomorrow.
I think supporting the other team members is essential in promoting a good team spirit.
Even though the clients had signed the contract and had agreed the specification, they asked for numerous modifications throughout the project.
Unfortunately, due to delays in technical testing, we're not going to meet the final deadline.
The consignment should be delivered by the end of the week.

Spelling
When spelling vocabulary in the field of projects and teams, remember:
- that *y* sometimes changes to *i* (*modify* (verb) → *modification* (noun)), but not when there is a vowel before the *y*:
  delay → *delays/delayed* (verb form)
  delay → *delays* (plural)
- irregular verbs: *see a project through* → *saw a project through*, *draw up a contract* → *drew up a contract*

- uncountable nouns have no plural form: *progress*
- verbs and nouns with –*ise* are often spelled –*ize* in US English: *to reorganise/reorganize*.

Pronunciation
When speaking, think about word stress.
- Notice how the stress within the following words stays the same for both the verb and the noun form:
  *to de**vel**op* → *de**vel**opment*
  *to re**qui**re* → *re**qui**rement*
- However, the stress within words sometimes changes between the verb and noun:
  *to pro**gress*** → *the **pro**gress*
  *to **mo**dify* → *a modification*
  *to re**or**ganize* → *reorgani**za**tion*
  *to pro**ject*** → ***pro**ject*

Also, there can be some differences in the way words are pronounced in US and UK English:
- The initial *sch* of *schedule* is pronounced /sk/ in the USA and /ʃ/ in the UK.
- *Project* is pronounced /ˈprəʊdʒekt/ in the USA and /ˈprɒdʒekt/ in the UK.

Collocations
Here are different verbs and nouns that can be used with some key vocabulary (in **bold**) relating to projects and teams.

to delay / postpone / push back **the start date**
to agree / sign / discuss / negotiate **a contract**
to agree / confirm / negotiate / extend **a deadline**
to draw up a schedule / contract / specifications
to (re)organize a meeting / schedule

Example
Our project manager, Véronique, had negotiated the contract and agreed the deadline with the client. She then drew up a schedule and organized a team meeting. However, due to unexpected recruitment delays, she had to delay the start date.

Word families
The table shows how some nouns and verbs in the area of projects and teams relate to one another.

noun	verb
delay	to delay
estimation	to estimate
leader	to lead
modification	to modify
organization	to organize
progress	to progress
proposal	to propose
schedule	to schedule
specification	to specify

Examples
*Following technical testing, we had to **modify** the design.* (verb)
*How much are the **modifications** going to cost? Are they worth doing?* (noun)
*The project manager wanted to **schedule** the entire production before attending the meeting with the clients.* (verb)
*At the meeting, the project manager presented the **schedule** to the clients for them to see what was realistic in the time available.* (noun)

Sales and marketing

Meaning
Here are some definitions and examples of vocabulary relating to sales and marketing.

to advertise – to encourage people to buy a product or service by writing about it (e.g. in a newspaper or on a website)

an advertisement – a notice on the Internet or in a magazine promoting a product or service

to appeal to – to be interesting for certain groups of people, such as young people or professional people

cold-calling – when salespeople call potential customers without prior arrangement to try and sell their products or services

a competitor – a company that makes the same product or provides the same service as you

a customer – someone who buys a product or service

to inquire – to ask about products or services on sale (also *to enquire*)

to launch an advertising campaign – to set a campaign in motion to promote products or services

to market products – to put products on the market; to sell

a potential customer – a possible new customer, not yet a customer but likely to be one

to promote goods – to advertise goods; to make them appealing to potential customers

promotional materials – materials such as brochures or websites used to promote and advertise items

to publicize – to make public; to advertise

a sales representative – a person responsible for selling products or services, who may travel to visit existing and potential customers

a trade fair – an exhibition of products or services in a particular field

> *Sales rep* is the short form for *sales representative*, and *ad* or *advert* is the short form for *advertisement*.

Examples
Some companies spend a lot of time on cold-calling.

When the sales rep went to visit a potential new customer, the customer inquired about delivery times.

After many months of planning, the advertising campaign was launched throughout Europe and North America.

There were plenty of promotional materials available to take away from the trade fair.

One of the key things is to appeal to your target customer base when promoting goods.

Spelling
When spelling vocabulary in the field of sales and marketing, remember:

- US English tends to use –ize and UK English generally uses –ise in many verbs and nouns: *to publicize/publicise, organization/organisation* (although you will often find –ize spellings in UK publications that are designed to appeal to an international audience). Note also that *advertise* is usually spelled with –ise in the USA as well as in the UK.
- that there are sometimes other spelling changes between US English and UK English: *to inquire/inquiry* (UK), *to enquire/enquiry* (US) (although both forms are found in UK English).
- some irregular verbs have a different spelling in the present tense and the past tense, but not all: *to come up with ideas* (came up with), *to take out an advert* (took out), *to sell products* (sold), *to set up a stand at a trade fair* (set up). (See page 80.)

- that a final *y* changes to *i* when the plural ending is added: *enquiry → enquiries*
- uncountable nouns do not have a plural form: *advertising, publicity, distribution, sales*

Pronunciation
- Notice the difference in stress patterns between these verb–noun pairs.
  *to **ad**vertise → ad**ver**tisement* (UK)
  *to **ad**vertise → adver**tise**ment* (US)
  *to **pub**licise/**pub**licize → pub**li**city*
  *to **de**monstrate → demon**stra**tion*
- Notice how sounds run together in the following phrases. This often happens when a consonant sound precedes a vowel sound.
  to set up   /tʌ/
  to take out   /kaʊ/
  to look into   /kɪ/
  to follow up   /wʌ/

Collocations
Here are different verbs and nouns that can be used with some key vocabulary (in **bold**) relating to sales and marketing.

to launch / run **an advertising campaign**
to agree / accept / negotiate **payment terms**
to attend / go to / organize **a trade fair**
to follow up an enquiry / a cold call / a meeting
to promote / advertise / publicize / sell / market **products**

Examples
We're hoping to run an advertising campaign when R&D have finished testing the new product.

Louise negotiated payment terms to within 21 days, which was an improvement of seven days on the existing arrangement.

CosyHome plc mainly markets its household products in northern Europe.

Word families
The table shows how some nouns, verbs and adjectives in the area of sales and marketing relate to one another.

noun	verb	adjective
ad advert advertisement	to advertise	advertised
distribution	to distribute	distributable
enquiry/inquiry	to enquire/inquire	
launch	to launch	
payment	to pay	payable
promotion	to promote	promotional
sales	to sell	saleable
publicity	to publicize	publicized, public

Examples
We can accept payment by cheque. Please make the cheque payable to SW Distribution Services.

The advertised sportswear sold better than we expected. We had put adverts in special sports magazines and in the leisure sections of national newspapers.

TransLogic's distribution costs are quite high. However, they do distribute throughout Asia and Australia, which appeals to many customers.

Telephoning and e-mailing

Meaning
Here are some definitions and examples of vocabulary relating to telephoning and e-mailing.

an addressee – a person to whom an e-mail or letter is addressed

an answerphone – a device connected to a phone (usually a landline) to record messages

to answer the (tele)phone – to take a call when the phone rings

an attachment – when you send a file or picture with an e-mail

a caller – a person who calls on the telephone

to call someone back – to phone someone who has left a message asking you to call them

a complaint – what you make when you are not satisfied with a service or product

confidential – describing information that is only for certain people

an enquiry – what someone makes when he/she asks for information

to forward – to pass an e-mail on to someone else

to get cut off – when the telephone connection is broken during a conversation

to get through – to be connected to the person you are calling on the phone

to give notification of (something) – to inform someone about something

good reception / a good signal – when the phone connection is very clear

to leave a message – to tell someone some information that needs to be passed on when you can't speak directly to the person you want

a landline – a telephone line that is connected to a particular building or department; not a mobile phone

to make a call – to telephone someone

to make an appointment – to arrange to meet someone

a mobile (phone) – a telephone that can be used on the move, in the street, etc.

to open an e-mail – to click on an e-mail to read it

a receiver – a handset of a phone

a recipient – a person who receives an e-mail or telephone call

to request information – to ask for information

to respond to an e-mail – to reply to an e-mail

a sender – a person who sends an e-mail

to take a message – to note down and (usually) pass on a message to the person the phone call was intended for

to text – to send an SMS message

voicemail – a built-in mechanism for recording messages on a phone

---

Note the difference between *receiver* and *recipient*.

Examples
I had a very good signal on my mobile phone, so I got through to Gillian straight away.
Beate's customer left a message while she was in a meeting, so she called him back as soon as she could.
I always check the sender before I open an e-mail attachment in case of a virus.
The e-mail was marked 'confidential', so the secretary forwarded it to the Head of Department.

Spelling
When spelling vocabulary in the field of telephoning and e-mailing, remember:
- that *y* sometimes changes to *i*:
  - verb → noun: *notify* → *notification*
  - plural: *enquiry* → *enquiries*
- irregular verbs: *get cut off* → *got cut off*, *leave a message* → *left a message*
- *i* before *e* except after *c*: *brief*, *receiver*
- UK and US English sometimes spell words differently:

UK	US
organise	*organize*
inquiry	*enquiry*

Pronunciation
The letter *t* can be pronounced in different ways:
- /t/ when the *t* is at the beginning, in the middle or at the end of a word: *telephone, attachment, cut*
- /θ/ when the *t* is followed by *h*, and the *th* is unvoiced: *thank, through*
- /ð/ when the *t* is followed by *h*, and the *th* is is voiced: *the, this*
- /ʃ/ when the *t* is part of the suffixes –*tion* or –*tial*: *reception, confidential*

Collocations
Here are different verbs and nouns that can be used with some key vocabulary (in **bold**) relating to telephoning and e-mailing.

to get a call / cut off / an e-mail / a message
to take a call / message
to make an appointment / a call

to cancel / change / keep / make / postpone **an appointment**
to delete / forward / reply to / send **an e-mail**
to answer / make / miss / receive **a telephone call**

Examples
I didn't get your message, sorry.
Sue had to keep the appointment, as she couldn't change it.
Why don't you forward the e-mail to me and I'll deal with it?
The sales rep made 20 calls in one morning.

Word families
The table shows how some nouns and verbs in the area of telephoning and e-mailing relate to one another.

noun	verb
address, addressee	to address
attachment	to attach
complaint	to complain
enquiry	to enquire
notification	to notify
recipient, reception, receiver	to receive
request	to request
response	to respond

Examples
*I'll **attach** the photo and send it as an **attachment**.* (verb, noun)
*I'm calling to **notify** you of the location for tomorrow's meeting.* (verb)
*He asked for **notification** in writing, so I'm sending him an e-mail.* (noun)
*Even though she was on a train, Cath had good mobile phone **reception** and was able to make and **receive** several calls on her journey.* (noun, verb)

VOCABULARY REFERENCE

Training

Meaning

Here are some definitions and examples of vocabulary relating to training.

assessment – when trainees are assessed or tested to see what they have learned

to attend – to take part in / participate in a training session or course

corporate training – training for businesses

a course coordinator – a person who coordinates and organizes training courses

course materials – the books, handouts, slides, etc. that a trainer may use during a training course

to develop skills – to improve and learn ideas and abilities to do things

to do well – to be able to put into practice what you have learned; to get good marks in a test

an exam – an official test that often leads to a qualification

to fail – to not do well enough to pass a test or exam

feedback – comments a trainer gives to the trainees to help them develop their skills further; information provided to the course organizer by the participants at the end of a course

government-funded training – training (partly) paid for by the government

to learn – to acquire new ideas and skills

lifelong learning – the concept of people continuing to learn throughout their careers and lives

marks – the results from a test or exam (e.g. 67%)

needs analysis – when trainees are asked what they need to learn

pressure – when trainees find a course difficult and feel under stress, especially if they need to pass an exam

a programme – what the training course covers; the content and timetable

to run a session – to hold/lead a session; to train

self-development – when people improve their skills by themselves, perhaps by reading a book rather than attending a course

a session – a specified time for training (there may be several sessions constituting a course)

to study – to take time to learn in a focused way

a skill – an ability and understanding of how to do something

to teach – to pass knowledge and skills onto someone else

a test – something given to learners to establish how much they have learned (usually more informal than an exam)

a trainee – a person who attends a training session or course

a trainer – a person who leads the training session or course

a workshop – a session often involving active participation (in contrast to a lecture)

> Notice the difference between *to learn* and *to teach*; and *trainee* and *trainer*.

> The word *training* on its own means the 'field of training', but people attend a training **course** or training **session**.

Examples

We are expecting 15 participants on the training course in May.
After carrying out a needs analysis of English language skills, the language school developed a programme of corporate training.
Peter was pleased with the marks he got in the computing skills test.
The aim of the workshop was to give participants the chance to do role-plays and receive feedback on how well they did in them.

Spelling

When spelling verbs in relation to training, remember:
- the spelling of irregular verbs in the past tense.

verb	past simple	past participle
take	took	taken
teach	taught	taught
learn	learnt/learned*	learnt/learned*
run	ran	run
find	found	found

- that regular verbs add –(e)d, and the letter *y* before the –(e)d changes to an *i*.

participate	participated	participated
study	studied	studied
fund	funded	funded**

* Both forms are correct, although *learned* is more common in US English.
** Notice the difference in spelling between the past forms of the verbs *to fund* (*funded*) and *to find* (*found*).

Pronunciation

The letter *s* can be pronounced:
- /s/ when the *s* occurs at the beginning of a word or after a consonant, or when it is doubled after a vowel (but not if it is also followed by a vowel): *study, assessment, marks*
- /z/ when the *s* occurs at the end of a word after a /d/ or /l/ sound, or between two vowels: *needs, skills, result*
- /ʃ/ when it is followed by *h*, or another *s* in the middle of a word before a vowel: *workshop, pressure, impression.*

Collocations

Here are different verbs that can be used with some key nouns (in **bold**) relating to training, and some adverbs that can be use with some key verbs (in **bold**).

to run **a session**, to develop **skills**, to take **an exam**, to have **a break**, to do **homework**, to give **feedback**, to get **results**

to study hard, **to do** well, **to do** badly, **to listen** attentively, **to participate** fully, **to take part in** a course willingly

Examples

Sarah took her exam in June and got her results in July.
The HR department is running a session on presentation skills.

Word families

The table shows how some nouns, verbs and adjectives in the area of training relate to one another.

noun	verb	adjective
assessment	to assess	assessed
learner	to learn	learned*
participant	to participate (in)	participatory
student	to study	studious
trainer, trainee	to train	trained

* Compare the pronunciation of the adjective /ˈlɜːnɪd/ with the past participle /lɜːnd/.

Examples

The student studied studiously.
Only trained trainers train.
The learned learner wanted to learn more.

Answer key

NEEDS ANALYSIS

Grammar

1 a 2 b 3 c 4 a 5 a 6 a 7 c 8 b 9 a 10 b 11 c
12 a 13 b 14 c 15 a 16 b 17 a 18 b 19 b 20 a
21 a 22 b 23 c 24 a

Vocabulary

1 a 2 b 3 a 4 b 5 a 6 a 7 b 8 b 9 a 10 c 11 c
12 a 13 b 14 a 15 b 16 a 17 c 18 b 19 c 20 c
21 a 22 c 23 c 24 a

GRAMMAR PRACTICE

Present tenses

1 1 Do you want 2 Do you often feel 3 provides 4 say
5 value 6 receive 7 Do you work 8 don't just offer
9 doesn't only involve 10 run 11 meets 12 finds

2 1 Are you giving 2 'm not doing 3 'm just leading
4 'm working 5 'm not planning 6 Are you doing
7 are you working 8 'm not managing
9 'm now running 10 is facing 11 're not selling
12 is changing 13 isn't keeping

3 1 Do you usually get a lift to work? (a)
2 Sally's just taking a tea break. (b)
3 We're not living in Manchester at the moment. (b)
4 Employees don't get pay rises very often. / Employees
don't very often get pay rises. (a)
5 Staff start work most days at 7.30 a.m. / Staff start work
at 7.30 a.m. most days. (a)
6 What is your boss doing right now? (b)

4 *Sample answers*
a We have a lunch break at 1 p.m. every day.
Project meetings are held at least twice month.
There is never any time to catch up on the admin.
b We're now looking at making staff redundant.
The Board of Directors is currently trying to draw up a
new business plan.
They're having a meeting this morning to discuss the
proposals.

5 1 *correct* (b)
2 I'**m working** in the finance department for a few days.
(a)
3 We'**re recruiting** for a new Marketing Manager at the
moment. (a)
4 My colleague's on leave, so I'**m handling** all his PR this
week. (a)
5 *correct* (a)
6 *correct* (b)
7 How many staff **do** you **have**? (b)
8 I **don't belong** to any union. (b)

6 1 a 2 d 3 c 4 e 5 b

7 1 are you doing 2 take 3 don't understand 4 use
5 're recruiting 6 do you come 7 isn't running
8 don't like

Past tenses

1 1 did; start 2 didn't finish 3 spent 4 enjoyed
5 increased 6 didn't cost 7 didn't complete 8 went

2 1 I'**ve worked** at Colourlines since January.
2 How long **have you** been a consultant?
3 *correct*
4 I'**ve earned** almost £1,000 in sales since June.
5 I'm sorry, I **haven't started** on the new project yet.
6 *correct*
7 How long **have** you **known** my boss?
8 My new employers haven't **contacted** me recently about
my starting date.

3 1 Sentence (a) implies that the holiday is over.
Sentence (b) implies that the holiday is not quite finished.
2 Sentence (a) implies that the speaker has no intention of
finishing the application.
Sentence (b) implies that the speaker will finish the
application at some point.
3 Sentence (a) implies that the speaker no longer works
overseas.
Sentence (b) implies that the speaker is still working
overseas.

4 1 b (A) 2 f (B) 3 e (A) 4 a (A) 5 d (B) 6 c (A)

5 1 last; already 2 ago; yet 3 for; already 4 since
5 ever; never 6 in; this
Past simple: put, received, did [you] join, sent
Present perfect: 've had, haven't had, has [only] worked,
's become, 've been, Have [you] been, 've [never] been,
've already done

6 1 haven't received 2 posted 3 got 4 told
5 hasn't written 6 came 7 's been 8 haven't heard
9 spoke 10 promised

Will and *going to*

1 1 're going to 2 won't he 3 Who's going 4 I'll
5 Are you going 6 Shall 7 I'll be 8 are we going to do

2 1 will you let 2 will begin 3 will be 4 won't last
5 will take 6 won't be 7 won't happen

3 1 b 2 f 3 d 4 a 5 c 6 e

4 *Sample answers*
2 I'll be at the dentist's tomorrow at 3 p.m..
3 Fraser will definitely finish the report by Friday
lunchtime.
4 My parents won't go on holiday to Italy next summer.
5 I won't be working in the same office in five years' time.

6 1 f 2 h 3 g 4 a 5 b 6 c 7 d 8 e

7 1 'll 2 'll 3 're going 4 'll 5 're going to
6 are you going to 7 'm going to 8 are going to 9 'll

Modals

1 1 May I ~~to~~ use your phone, please?

    2 You don't have **to** come to the exhibition.

    3 *correct*

    4 Jack **could** help us, I think.

    5 My boss doesn't ~~can~~ speak French. (*or* ~~doesn't~~ **can't** speak)

    6 You shouldn't **be** working here so late. (*or* shouldn't **work**)

    7 I **can't** ring my boss now; he's already left.

    8 *correct*

2 1 Shall I pick you up later?

    2 Could you repeat that, please?

    3 May I sit here, please?

    4 Can I speak to Jane, please?

    5 May I interrupt you for a moment?

    6 Shall I order a taxi?

4 2 Do you have to work until 6 p.m.?

    3 They don't have to send the report off today.

    4 All staff must sign in before 8 a.m.

    5 You mustn't tell anyone about the new contract – it's a secret.

    6 You mustn't forget to ask Maggie about the meeting.

5 2 May/Could/Can I spend some money from the department's budget, please?

    3 May/Could/Can I take a day off next week, please?

    4 May/Could/Can I use your computer, please?

    5 May/Could/Can I use your office for a while, please?

    6 May/Could/Can I take a short break, please?

7 *Sample answers*

    1 ... should finish this tomorrow.

    2 ... should worry about it too much.

    3 ... should buy it.

    4 ... should look for another one?

    5 ... should look at hiring a coach.

    6 ... should apply?

8 1 should 2 Could 3 can't 4 Shall 5 may 6 might
7 couldn't

Conditionals

1 1 c (1) 2 b (2) 3 f (1) 4 d (2) 5 a (1) 6 e (2)

2 1 'll stay 2 doesn't 3 might come; don't 4 takes
5 won't be; don't 6 will help; ask

3 1 're; will sack 2 'll go; don't hurry 3 see; 'll give
4 'll stop; 're 5 don't leave; 'll miss 6 will improve; go
7 don't read; won't understand

4 1 'd study 2 'd put 3 'd go; had 4 offered 5 tried
6 wouldn't attend; didn't enjoy 7 would shop; reduced
8 lived; 'd need

5 1 built 2 would 3 be 4 moved 5 make 6 might

6 *Sample answers*

    If I lost my job, I'd start up my own business.

    If the price of petrol rose substantially, I'd sell my car.

    If I failed my examinations, I'd retake them next year.

    If I missed my bus to work, I'd take a taxi.

    If I saw someone steal in a shop, I'd call the police.

7 *Sample answers*

    2 If I was/were you, I'd send out some colourful marketing flyers.

    3 If I was/were you, I'd speak to his manager.

    4 If I was/were you, I'd take on some more admin staff.

    5 If I was/were you, I'd organize a social event, like a barbecue.

8 1 If you ~~will~~ want help, Janet will assist you.

    2 *correct*

    3 What would you do if your boss **made** you redundant?

    4 If all the staff ~~will~~ book flights together, they get a discount.

    5 I**'ll come** and see you later in the office if I have time.

    6 *correct*

    7 *correct*

    8 If I **was/were** you, I'd tell your boss about your concerns with the project.

    9 We won't finish this report if we **don't** do it today.

    10 We wouldn't come to the meeting even if you **invited** us.

–ing forms + infinitives

1 1 c 2 f 3 e 4 a 5 d 6 b

2 1 to take 2 to pay 3 to turn 4 to meet 5 to check
6 to get

3 2 My friend wanted me to get the promotion.

    3 Our boss told us not to tell anyone about the staff changes.

    4 We were warned to expect further redundancies next year.

    5 My colleague reminded me (not to forget) to post that letter.

    6 You were warned not to be late.

4 1 to do 2 to concentrate 3 to work 4 to see 5 to sit
6 to bring

5 1 in attending 2 of talking 3 about losing
4 on writing 5 at making 6 before going

6 1 Do you enjoy playing badminton in your free time?

    2 I suggest going home.

    3 Stop making that noise!

    4 I don't mind working late.

    5 We need to keep promoting the product.

    6 Have you finished writing the article?

7 1 Spending has gone down on electrical goods. / Spending on electrical goods has gone down.

    2 Making time for appraisals will be impossible.

    3 Waiting for the meeting to start was boring.

    4 The best part of my role is managing staff.

    5 Understanding cultural differences is key to international business.

8 1 to give 2 chairing 3 having 4 holding 5 writing
6 working 7 to help 8 to go 9 managing 10 Working

Comparatives and superlatives

1 1 Is it **easier** to take the train or drive?

2 Which is the **most** successful product out of these three?

3 Your TV is more **modern** than mine.

4 This car is less efficient **than** my previous one.

5 Is your role the same **as** mine?

6 Our office is much **bigger** now.

2 1 nearer   2 than   3 bit   4 more   5 further   6 expensive

3 1 bigger   2 more difficult   3 more helpful
4 more interesting   5 less complicated

4 1 the oldest   2 the best   3 the most modern   4 the funniest
5 the smallest   6 the lowest

5 1 Lema is the least creative member of staff.

2 London is the biggest city in England.

3 Your report is the most comprehensive I've read.

4 My job is the least interesting here.

5 Sales are at their lowest since 1999.

6 1 more sharply   2 more quickly   3 more dramatically
4 the slowest   5 more cheaply

7 2 The BriefU project is less important to us than the Xtra
project.

3 People in London spend about the same amount of time
on paperwork as (people) in Berlin.

4 My computer isn't as efficient as Sally's.

5 Not as many people are taking part in training as ten
years ago.

8 1 better   2 complicated   3 hard(er)   4 worst
5 more organized   6 the most reliable   7 well

Relative clauses

1 a 1, 2, 4, 7, 8

b 3, 5, 6

c 2, 8

d 1, 7, 8

2 1 Joseph, who lives in Birmingham, works in the HR
department.

2 Marian Cavender, whose team is based in New York, is
taking early retirement.

3 Kris, who runs the logistics department, is thinking of
setting up his own business.

3 1 that   2 that   3 who   4 which   5 whose   6 who
7 which   8 that

4 2 Britta, who comes from Sweden, has just been made
Production Manager.

3 The printer, which cost $1m, has helped us to extend our
business.

4 John, whose car has broken down, has become Head of
Department.

5 Our new software, which was expensive, has enabled us
to improve our company's systems.

6 Nadja, whose colleague is off sick, is leading today's
meeting.

7 The offices, which are very old, are located in Coventry
city centre.

8 Petra, who is often late for work, is the lead organizer for
the annual conference.

5 1 Sentence (a) implies that there may be more than one
printer, but it is the one that was bought last month that
has broken down twice.
Sentence (b) implies that there is only one printer (which
was bought last month) and it has broken down twice.

2 Sentence (a) implies that out of a number of staff
members, there are two who are based in California.
Sentence (b) implies that there are only two staff
members in total, and both of them are based in
California.

6 The relative pronoun can be left out in 3, 4 and 5.

7 1 I've found out the names of those employees **who/that**
will need to move offices.

2 *correct*

3 The fax to Thorns, **which** I should have sent yesterday,
is still on my desk.

4 *correct*

5 The software which I ordered it hasn't arrived yet.

6 Joona, who is our latest recruit, used to work for GOAL.

7 *correct*

8 Jakob's the person **whose** computer was found damaged.

Articles

1 1 a   2 a   3 an   4 a   5 an   6 a   7 a   8 an   9 a   10 a

2 1 We've launched **a**(**nother**) new product.

2 My brother works as **a** teacher.

3 Are you **an** operator or **a** receptionist?

4 It's **a** very exciting project.

5 That was **a** lovely cup of coffee. Can I have **another** cup?

3 1 f (–)   2 h (–)   3 c (–)   4 a (the)   5 e (the)   6 d (the)
7 b (the)   8 g (–)

4 1 *correct*

2 Is your office in **the** city centre?

3 *correct*

4 My favourite programme, *Business Time*, is on **the** radio
tonight.

5 My uncle used to be in **the** police.

6 Our company is **the** biggest in the sector.

7 My line manager and I live in **the** same street.

8 I'd like my computer to go on **the** left of the desk.

9 What's **the** time, please?

10 *correct*

5 2 Sentence (a) implies that the mobile was found by
chance, and wasn't a particular mobile.
Sentence (b) implies that the mobile was a specific one
that the speaker was looking for.

3 Sentence (a) implies that there is already a new
computer, and Tara needs it.
Sentence (b) implies that Tara needs a replacement for
her old computer.

4 Sentence (a) implies that there is music currently playing
in reception and that you love it.
Sentence (b) implies that you love the idea of music
playing in reception, although that is not necessarily
happening at the moment.

5 Sentence (a) implies either that there were several large
tables, or that the table had not been previously
mentioned.
Sentence (b) implies that there is only one large table.

6 Sentence (a) doesn't ask about a particular job.
Sentence (b) asks about one job in particular.

6 1 the   2 a   3 a   4 the   5 –   6 the   7 the   8 the   9 –
10 the   11 a   12 the   13 an   14 the   15 –   16 –

Determiners

1

countable singular	countable plural	uncountable
leaflet, lorry, manager, suggestion, warehouse	employees, euros, offices	advice, energy, finance, information, marketing

2 1 some   2 any   3 some   4 any   5 any   6 any   7 some
8 any   9 some   10 any

3 1 Sentence (a) implies that there were hardly any people
there.
Sentence (b) implies that there were some people there.

2 Sentence (a) implies that you speak hardly any English.
Sentence (b) implies that you speak some English.

4 1 few mistakes   2 a few reports   3 a little milk
4 few hotels   5 a few; people   6 little unemployment
7 little time   8 a little petrol   9 a few; suggestions

5 1 many   2 much   3 a lot of   4 much   5 a lot of   6 lots of
7 many   8 many   9 a lot of   10 lots of

6 1 any   2 a few   3 some   4 little   5 some   6 a lot of
7 a few   8 some   9 anything   10 a few   11 some

Passives

1 1, 3, 4, 5, 6 are passives.

2 1 A leading London accountant was **elected** to a senior
post within the industry.

2 An established insurance firm, which **is located** to the
north of Warsaw, has gone bankrupt.

3 MK Vehicles has **been** taken over by its rivals.

4 It is **expected** that staff at R Media will receive a pay
increase of 4%.

5 A project aimed at helping companies become more
competitive **has** been launched by SMT Finance Group.

3 1 a   2 b   3 a   4 a
The more formal sentences use the passive.

4 2 The applicants will be interviewed next week by the HR
Manager.

3 The/A seminar is currently being organized by the
Training Director.

4 The/A presentation was given yesterday by Jon.

5 £1,000 has already been spent on software by the IT
Assistant.

6 An eco-friendly taxi might be developed by a Coventry
company in the next two years.

5 1 are   2 sent   3 been   4 will   5 have   6 is   7 given

6 1 Two members of staff have been promoted.

2 While Jack is on leave, the invoices will be signed off (by
someone else).

3 The new *Inspire me* DVD was launched yesterday.

4 Every Friday, timesheets are sent to Finance.

7 Exhibitors from around the world have **been** invited to take
part in the country's largest flooring trade show. Over 140
firms have already booked space at the Big Floor Fair, which
is being organized by Erkki OY. The three-day event will
bring together importers, exporters, manufacturers and
wholesalers. Show spokesman Peter Laing said: 'Last year's
show **was** attended by over 1,000 delegates – but I think
that record will be **broken** this year! An advert for the
show **was** placed in a national newspaper three weeks ago,
and we have already received twice as many enquiries as
this time last year.'

Reported speech

1 1 b   2 e   3 a   4 c   5 d

2 1 Markus said (that) staff morale wasn't very good.

2 Benjamin said (that) job losses were highly likely.

3 I told my boss I'd finished all my tasks.

4 Jacky said she couldn't attend the team meeting.

5 My boss said (that) sales would rise over the next three
months.

6 Carole said (that) the photocopier didn't work.

7 She said she didn't like working weekends.

8 We said we didn't know why the office was so cold.

3 1 He denied wanting Jenny to resign.

2 My colleague suggested travelling to the conference
together.

3 My boss recommended staying at the May Hotel.

4 Sheila mentioned going to a good conference in Milan
last year / the previous year.

5 Gerard reported finding a few problems with the budget.

6 The new operative admitted (to) switching off the
machine.

4 1 My assistant refused to write the report for me.

2 A colleague offered (to give) me a lift to the station.

3 Cecile agreed to give the presentation the following
month.

4 My boss promised to finish the summary by Friday.

5 Two staff members decided to leave.

6 My boss wanted me to arrange a meeting the following
week.

5 1 give   2 ask   3 advised   4 you   5 to do   6 me
7 to cancel

6 1 the next/following day   2 before/previously
3 then / at that time   4 the day before

7 1 to check her e-mails

2 me to open any post addressed to her

3 to deal promptly with any orders

4 getting / that I get help from you / asking you for help

5 didn't want

6 me to process them as they came in

7 thought there would be a few bills to deal with

8 didn't know exactly when she would be back

VOCABULARY PRACTICE

Companies and offices

1 1 expanding   2 recognized   3 base   4 environment   5 hot
6 merged

2 1 took over   2 merging   3 internationally recognized/
recognised   4 competitive   5 reputation   6 security

3 2 A good reputation requires hard work.

3 RJ Chemicals is recognized internationally.

4 Take the lift to the third floor.

5 The takeover resulted in job losses.

6 A clean and friendly working environment is important
to me.

7 We work solely with well-known companies.

8 We support upcoming companies in their development.

4 *Sample answers*

upcoming company, well-known company, internationally
recognized company, multinational company

modern office, open-plan office, old-fashioned office

5 1 profit   2 profitable   3 expansion   4 to expand
5 reputation   6 reputable   7 merger   8 to merge
9 to compete   10 competitive   11 to trade   12 trading

Finance

1 1 total sales figures   2 exact figure (at past point)
3 to be up by 30%   4 to drop   5 to even out
6 rough figure (at future point)   7 to nose-dive   8 to rocket
9 short-term outlook   10 long-term outlook

2 1 economic   2 instability   3 unprofitable   4 predict
5 financial   6 rates   7 investment   8 share

3

/ɒ/ as in cost	/əʊ/ as in overdraft	/ɔː/ as in shortage
drop	loans	board meeting
profit	nose-dive	forecast
rocket	overheads	foresee
	total sales figures	

4 *Sample answers*

exact figures, rough figures, to finalize figures, to double-
check figures, to chase up figures, total (sales) figures, long-
term figures, to predict (sales) figures, to look into (sales)
figures

5 1 a rise   2 to increase   3 to drop   4 a fall   5 to decrease
6 a nose-dive

Human resources

1 1 b   2 a   3 e   4 f   5 c   6 d

2 1 job application   2 appraisee   3 employer   4 redundancy
5 pension   6 development

3

ooOo	oO	oOo
application	apply recruit employ	recruitment appraisal employer

ooO	Ooo	Oo
appraisee employee	salary company	notice

4 1 recruitment; vacant   2 sick leave   3 union; company
4 staff   5 skills; training   6 apply; advertising

5 1 application/applicant   2 applicable   3 redundant
4/5/6 employer/employee/employment   7 employable
8 recruitment/recruiter   9 to recruit   10 to appraise
11 to develop

Logistics

1

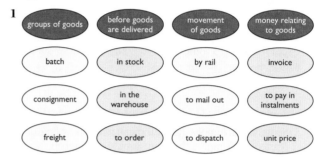

2 1 consignment   2 freight   3 invoice   4 instalments
5 supplied   6 deliveries

3

	/tʃ/ as in chair	/ʃ/ as in shop
shipment		✓
dispatch	✓	
purchase	✓	
confirmation		✓
batch	✓	
insurance		✓
financial		✓
check	✓	

4 *Sample answers*

transport costs / delays / problems / strategy

to transport freight / goods / a consignment / by road /
by rail

5 1 carefully   2 considerably   3 directly   4 fast
5 immediately   6 slowly   7 speedily   8 swiftly

Meetings and conferences

1 1 c   2 b   3 d   4 a

2 1 c   2 e   3 a   4 b   5 d   6 f

3 1 appointment   2 questionnaire   3 minutes   4 negotiate
5 photocopy   6 videoconference

4 1 presenter   2 organize   3 cancel   4 write up a report
5 agree   6 book a venue   7 projector   8 attendance

5 1 reach; postpone   2 fill in; take   3 write up
4 book; cancel   5 take   6 attend; hold; postpone; cancel;
book; arrange   7 make; postpone; cancel   8 make
(Note: we do not say *take a report* in the sense of writing the
notes for a report, although we say *take the minutes*.)

6 1 disagreement   2 postponement   3 attendance
4 organization   5 presentation   6 negotiator   7 booking
8 participant   9 discussion   10 speaker

People and places

1 1 d 2 a 3 e 4 b 5 c

2 1 a 2 d 3 b 4 e 5 c

3 1 overlooking 2 head; outskirts 3 location; access
4 based in 5 subordinate 6 colleagues 7 partner
8 secretary

4

/eɪ/ as in **pay**	/eə/ as in **trade _fair_**	/æ/ as in **manu-_facture_**	/ɑː/ as in **_farther_**	/ə/ as in **_attend_**
based in industrial estate location sales manager	warehouse	factory manager	partner	assistant central subor-dinate

5 1 distribution, development, training, financial, call

2 pretty, central, easily accessible, industrial, rural

3 sales, team, finance, distribution, development, training

4 sales, distribution, development, training, finance

6 1 manager 2 buyer 3 assistant 4 sales manager
5 lawyer 6 trainer 7 scientist 8 economist 9 engineer

Planning

1 1 plan 2 diversify 3 predict 4 risk 5 able 6 targets
7 achievable 8 goal 9 vision 10 strategy

2 1 analyzing 2 diversified 3 strategies 4 drawn up
5 enabling 6 set

3

	pronounced /r/	not pronounced
risk	✓	
fo**r**ecast		✓
cu**rr**ently	✓	
p**r**edict	✓	
realistic	✓	
dive**r**sify		✓
failu**r**e		✓
conce**r**n		✓

Note: There are some regional accents where the *r* may be pronounced in the middle of a word, e.g. *diversify*.

4 1 We need to *draw **up** strategies*.

2 Long-term *plans were **drawn** up* at the last Board meeting.

3 *correct*

4 David is working with an external agency to ***set** targets* for the whole department.

5 *correct*

6 I'm only interested in hearing about ***achievable** goals*, not unrealistic ones.

5 1 cautiously 2 immediate 3 realistic 4 unrealistic
5 optimistically 6 ambitious

Production and processes

1 1 shifts 2 supplier 3 test 4 schedule 5 unit 6 install
7 QA 8 trial run

2 1 implemented; procedure 2 consignments 3 production
4 schedule 5 supplier; delivery 6 quality 7 stock
8 maintenance 9 assurance

3 1 a **pro**cess 2 to in**stall** 3 instal**la**tion 4 a **pro**duct
5 to pro**duce** 6 a **ware**house

4 1 b 2 a 3 e 4 c 5 d

5 2 to maintain 3 to update 4 to schedule 5 to produce
6 to purchase 7 to supply 8 to deliver

Projects and teams

1 1 a 2 b 3 a 4 a 5 a 6 b

2 1 schedule 2 brief 3 consignment 4 postpone
5 modifications 6 reorganize (Note that UK English sometimes spells this *reorganise*.)

3

Oo	oO	oOo
progress project schedule	postpone progress project	requirements
Ooo	**oOoo**	**oooOo**
customer	developments reorganize	modifications specifications

4 *Progress* and *project* both have the stress pattern Oo as a noun and oO as a verb.

5 1 delay 2 work with 3 confirm 4 sign 5 make
6 deliver

6 2 to lead a project 3 to reorganize the team
4 to confirm a deadline 5 to schedule 6 to modify
7 to specify 8 to estimate costs 9 to delay

Sales and marketing

1 1 a 2 e 3 f 4 d 5 c 6 b

2 1 organized 2 enquiries 3 sets up / is setting up
4 inquiring 5 (has) sold 6 publicise

3 1 His job is to look into attracting new customers.

2 Head Office has decided to set up a new distribution centre.

3 It is good practice to follow up cold calls with written confirmation.

4 Why not take out an advert to promote sales?

5 You could sell on the Internet.

6 We hope to move into markets overseas.

4 1 followed up 2 attend 3 market 4 agree 5 launching
6 promote

5 1 distribution, enquiry, launch, payment/payee, promotion, publicity, sales

2 enquiry (inquiry), publicize (publicise)

3 distribution, publicity, sales

Telephoning and e-mailing

1 1 get through   2 leave; message; answerphone; voicemail
3 cut off   4 attachment   5 forward   6 confidential
7 appointment   8 complaint

2 1 recipient   2 addressee/address   3 to forward   4 *correct*
5 *correct*   6 *correct*   7 complaint   8 *correct*   9 *correct*
10 confidential   11 receiver   12 attachment
Note: *enquiry* can also be spelled *inquiry* and *organize* can
also be spelled *organise*.

3

/t/ as in <u>t</u>able	/θ/ as in <u>th</u>ink	/ð/ as in <u>th</u>en	/ʃ/ as in loca<u>ti</u>on
answer the telephone take text notification cut off recipient attachment	thank get through	answer the telephone address the sender	reception confidential notification

4 1 get   2 take   3 make

5 *Sample answers*

1 make/cancel/postpone/change/confirm

2 write/type/send/receive/forward/reply to/delete

3 receive/make/miss/answer

6 1 attach   2 receive   3 receive   4 receive   5 address
6 notify   7 request   8 complain   9 enquire   10 respond

Training

1 1 materials   2 test   3 run   4 attend   5 skills   6 learn
7 result(s)   8 needs   9 exam   10 teach   11 study
12 breaks   13 marks   14 sessions

2 1 attended, have attended
2 took part, have taken part
3 participated, have participated
4 trained, have trained
5 taught, have taught
6 learnt/learned, have learnt/learned
7 studied, have studied
8 ran, have run
9 funded, have funded
10 did well, have done well
11 failed, have failed
12 gave feedback, have given feedback

3

/s/ as in <u>s</u>tudy	/z/ as in feel<u>s</u>	/ʃ/ as in <u>sh</u>ow
session course materials skills self-development test marks stress needs analysis assessment results	course materials skills needs analysis results	session workshop pressure

4 1 run   2 develop   3 do   4 take   5 have   6 do   7 give
8 get

5 1 hard   2 well   3 badly   4 attentively   5 fully   6 quickly
7 willingly   8 enthusiastically

6 1 to study, student   2 to participate, participant
3 to train, trainee/trainer   4 to learn, learner
5 to assess, assessment/assessor

SOME COMMON IRREGULAR VERBS

Present	Past	Past participle
be	was, were	been
become	became	become
begin	began	begun
break	broke	broken
bring	brought	brought
build	built	built
buy	bought	bought
choose	chose	chosen
come	came	come
cut	cut	cut
do	did	done
drink	drank	drunk
drive	drove	driven
eat	ate	eaten
fall	fell	fallen
feel	felt	felt
find	found	found
forget	forgot	forgotten
get	got	got(ten)
give	gave	given
go	went	gone
grow	grew	grown
have	had	had
hear	heard	heard
hide	hid	hidden
hold	held	held
keep	kept	kept
know	knew	known
lead	led	led
leave	left	left
lose	lost	lost
make	made	made
meet	met	met
pay	paid	paid
read /riːd/	read /red/	read /red/
run	ran	run
say	said	said
see	saw	seen
sell	sold	sold
send	sent	sent
sing	sang	sung
sit	sat	sat
sleep	slept	slept
speak	spoke	spoken
spend	spent	spent
stand	stood	stood
steal	stole	stolen
take	took	taken
teach	taught	taught
tell	told	told
think	thought	thought
understand	understood	understood
wear	wore	worn
win	won	won
write	wrote	written